BEGINNER'S GUIDE

Painting Flowers

JENNY RODWELL

STUDIO VISTA

ACKNOWLEDGEMENTS

The author and publishers would like to thank the following artists who have allowed us to use their work in this book: Edward Bishop, p. 7; Charmian Edgerton, pp. 62–3, 66–7; Alan Halliday, pp. 6–7; Audrey Hammond, pp. 8–9; David Hutter, pp. 6, 20–1; Sally Michel, pp. 21, 63; Jack Millar, pp. 9, 49; Salliann Putnam, pp. 4–5. Special thanks to Charmian Edgerton, Ian Sidaway, Adrian Paschal Smith and Stan Smith for their step-by-step demonstrations and artwork; and to Fred Munden for taking the photographs.

Studio Vista
an imprint of
Cassell
Villiers House
41/47 Strand
London WC2N 5JE

First published 1993

British Library Cataloguing in Publication Data
A catalogue record for this book is available from the British Library

ISBN 0-289-80081-1

Series editors: Jenny Rodwell and Patricia Monahan
The moral rights of the author have been asserted

Series designer Edward Pitcher

Distributed in the United States by
Sterling Publishing Co. Inc.
387 Park Avenue South, New York, NY 10016-8810

Typeset by Litho Link Ltd, Welshpool, Powys, Wales
Printed in Great Britain by
Bath Colourbooks, Glasgow

CONTENTS

CHAPTER 1 CHAPTER

Painting plants and flowers

FORGET YOU ARE looking at a flower. What stands before you, as you set out on the fascinating trail of flower painting, is not only a bunch of daffodils, say, or a rose. It is also an array of shapes, colours and tones, often set against a background of more shapes, colours and tones.

Using this book, you can 'see' and portray nature. You will be able to escape the trap into which many fall when they try to depict flowers and plants: the tendency to feel restricted to a small-scale, meticulous representation. With the aid of practical step-by-step projects by professional artists, we demonstrate that flower painting is a much broader art than many realize, with a rich variety of approaches and materials available, including oils, water-colours, collage and pastels. All the projects included here are accessible, and you follow the artist's progress through to the final picture.

The book simplifies the techniques required to paint the organic, growing forms of living flowers and plants. It shows how to capture the essence of dynamic, growing structures in broad terms, but it also helps you achieve the more specific, naturalistic effects.

Paint flowers just as you would paint any other subject. In other words, forget you are painting a flower or a plant, and look at the subject as if you were seeing it for the first time. Don't worry about specific stalks, leaves and petals. Artist Salliann Putman, who painted this arrangement of wild flowers, thinks of her subject purely in terms of shape, colour and form. 'I'm a painter, not a botanist. Sometimes I don't even know the names of the flowers I paint.'

FLOWERS UNLIMITED

The variety is enormous. The flowers of Matisse (1869–1954) often appear in giant paintings or collages, based on huge cut-out petal and leaf motifs, brought together to satisfy his fascination with design and pure colour. The huge canvases of Monet (1840–1926), who was a gardener as well as an artist, show flowers growing in their natural surroundings. On the other hand, many artists worked on a much smaller scale, producing meticulous drawings and paintings of flowers and plants for botanical books.

These widely different approaches, from the flamboyant to the scientifically precise, demonstrate a wide, exciting world beyond the confines of the rather narrow, dainty works which so often spring to mind when we think of flower painting. The flower painter is by no means restricted to a 'pretty picture' of cut flowers in a vase – although many lovely works have been produced by those understandably attracted to the inherent prettiness of the subject. It is easy to forget that flower paintings can be as individual as the artists who paint them.

Flowers are the most versatile of subjects and there is no reason why they should not be treated in exactly the same way as any other subject.

Canvas to cushion

Nothing could be less dainty than Matisse's brilliant, decorative works. Sometimes the flat shapes are arranged realistically, so that we can actually see a bunch of flowers, ceramic pot or white jug in the picture. At other times, Matisse chooses to use the floral motifs in a purely decorative and fanciful way, creating dancing patterns of coloured shapes which often stand out strikingly against a bright-white background.

Profuse colour

More naturalistic, but equally adventurous, is the work of the Impressionist Claude Monet, whose flower paintings are about sunlight and colour. Monet often had several paintings on the go at any particular time, moving from one enormous canvas to another as the sun moved across the sky. So

◁ **Pansies in a glass vase** *As with most of his watercolour flower paintings, artist David Hutter keeps the subject and composition very simple. The painting is divided into two main shapes, the tabletop and the darker background; the flowers are loosely painted over a light, accurate line drawing.*

◁ **Tulips on a lace cloth** *In this watercolour, Alan Halliday combines flower painting with still-life, taking colour and design as the main elements. To emphasize these, the subject is viewed from above; linear perspective and constructed space are virtually eliminated from the composition.*

every day the sun was in the same place and the light was always consistent for the picture he was working on.

Like Monet, you can portray flowers as shimmering smudges of glowing, vibrating pigment. Seen from close quarters, the blooms may be unrecognizable. Viewed from some distance, Monet's smudges come together and we see hollyhocks and lupins in the herbaceous border, dandelions and daisies on the sunlit lawn, and waterlilies merging with their own reflections in the garden pond.

Art and science

Quite a different type of flower painter works with an almost technical precision. This is the botanical artist, whose interest in the subject is far more exacting and specific. The purpose here is usually to record and convey accurate information rather than to create a personal impression of what is seen.

Since the sixteenth century botanical artists have travelled round the world with explorers and scientists, using their skills to document rare and unknown species in the lands they visited. In the days before photography their drawings and paintings had to be accurate, for this was the only way of showing the world what the newly discovered flowers and plants looked like.

Most of us are quite unaware of the structural parts that make up a plant, let alone the scientific terms used to describe them. Monet in his garden and Matisse in his studio were probably not worrying about the Latin names of the flowers they painted, but they certainly looked just as carefully at the shapes and structures as the artists who did. Only in this way could they retain and convey the character of the flowers in their work.

▷ **Balcony in the sun** *A vase of flowers by an open door plays a small but important role in this interior scene painted in oils by Edward Bishop. The colours and shapes of the indoor flowers are echoed by those in the garden beyond, giving a sense of scale and space to the picture.*

FINE OR CHUNKY

If you like working on a huge scale with chunky pastel or charcoal, then do so. If you prefer using big paintbrushes to small ones, go ahead. Flowers may appear to be fine and fragile subjects, but they do not necessarily have to be painted that way.

In fact, chunky materials are often better because they help overcome a common beginner's problem: that of getting too involved with detail at the expense of the overall image.

Flowers and plants constitute a subject which gives you a vast range of colour, size and shape to choose from. Obviously the selection changes through the year, but this means there is always something new to paint, always a fresh subject waiting to replace the one you have just finished.

Flowers in landscape

A narrow line divides some flower paintings from what would normally be described as landscape work. Flowers painted in their natural environment, whether this is a field, a garden, a park or a window-box, cannot easily be separated from the surrounding scenery. And you can often make the picture more interesting by including other elements.

A field of daisies will probably include the sky or some distant hills; a garden painting could be set against a wall or building. In this landscape context, space becomes an important part of a painting. One pleasant aspect of this is that you can take your materials out into the open air and enjoy the sense of space that surrounds the subject.

The Victorians were fond of painting their own gardens, showing off the flowers in great detail. Often they included a garden path, a wall or even the house in the background, with the colourful flowers and foliage showing up beautifully against the warm, neutral tones of brick and stonework.

Although some of these 'cottage garden' paintings may be rather too quaint for modern tastes, the artists were often highly successful in bringing together different elements in one composition. Gardens today are simpler; the massed blooms of the old traditional cottage gardens are more likely to be found in parks and botanical gardens, but they are still there, accessible to all, and just as colourful.

Still life with flowers

The majority of flower paintings are done indoors, with the flowers or plants arranged specially for the painting. In this context, the flower painting becomes a still life and you can arrange the flowers or plants to your own liking. You can choose the setting and background, and bring as many other objects into the picture as you wish.

A painting begins long before you actually get out your paints and pencils; it starts at the planning stage and with the choice of subject, so do take advantage of all the options. A simple study of a single flower or flowers in a vase can be stunning, but it is not the only possibility.

▷ **Flowers as still-life** *In this oil painting by Jack Millar, the jugs, tablecloth and background are as important as the plants and flowers. It is a still-life arrangement – a composition of shapes, textures, colour and light.*

▽ **Flowers with figure** *'Thomas Asleep' by Audrey Hammond is a painting of the artist's son, with flowers and other objects dominating the foreground. The painting is done in poster colour and black ink; the approach is bold, with strong shapes laid in broad strokes of intense colour.*

Albrecht Dürer (1471–1528), one of the first and most influential of all flower painters, was also a master of still life. His paintings are remarkable not just for the care and colour that go into each individual flower, but also for the imaginative way in which the flowers are arranged and embellished. The formality of a basket of roses, tulips, marigolds and lilies of the valley is offset by the fact that some of the flowers are strewn around on the table top; a bee nestles at the heart of a white rose; and a red admiral butterfly crawls up the stem of a pink and white tulip.

Plants and flowers need not be painted in isolation unless particularly desired. You can introducc different colours, textures and shapes into a composition by bringing in other objects. Butterflies and bees were Dürer's way, but on a more practical level you can arrange plants and flowers with fruit; in a domestic setting; on a windowsill with a landscape behind them; and against a variety of different backgrounds – plain, patterned, light or dark. Think of the rich possibilities; don't just thrust your bunch of daffs into any old pot and sit down to paint them.

FORMS OF NATURE

Natural form is often beautiful – which is why it attracts the artist – but it can be full of surprises once we start to look at it as a subject for a painting. We find that we have been looking at nature without actually seeing it, because our brains tend to view things in a rapid, overall way in order to place them quickly into useful categories.

Even one single flower can be daunting when we want to draw or paint it. It has a complex structure and is very fragile. It is made of seemingly simple petals, yet each petal has many planes. Worse still, being so familiar, it can be difficult to 'see' with fresh eyes.

The first thing to remember is that you will not usually want to capture every detail of the flower. Normally, a flower or plant will be one part of a larger painting, and will possibly be painted in quite a general or minimal way. But however minimal the painted flower – even if it is a single stroke of colour representing, say, a bluebell in a wood – it must be accurate. And this means you have to look carefully at the real flower.

Like most things in nature, flowers and leaves can be viewed in a special way which will help you to simplify them in order to draw or paint them.

Learning to analyse

Although nothing in the plant world is absolutely regular or geometric, almost everything has an underlying geometric form. Try, if you can, not to copy what you see but rather to analyse and simplify the structure of the subject in front of you. The studies here show how various flower and plant forms can be 'broken down' into basic forms.

Take, for instance, a fairly straightforward subject like a bunch of daisies. Such a simple little flower, yet with so many petals and leaves that it is difficult to know where to begin!

A good starting point is to do as the artist has done in this example. Forget about the petals for the time being, and position the flowers correctly in relation to each other. The flower heads are not

◁ **Drawing flowers** *Flowers and plants are easier to draw if you first see them as simple geometric forms. Before starting, the artist made a pencil drawing, positioning and constructing each flower in its simplest form.*

actually circular, but they are close enough for you to be able to treat each one as a flat, circular shape, or an ellipse if you are looking at it sideways.

These simple shapes can be rubbed out and corrected until everything is the right shape and in the right place. When you are happy with this, you can develop the flowers as the artist has done here.

Leaves will always look more realistic if you understand how they are growing. Do they grow from the stem in alternate pairs? Do they grow from the base of the stem? Are they wrapped around the stem? Looking and understanding are often the most important parts of drawing, and this is especially true with plants and flowers.

Space and perspective

Plants and flowers are three-dimensional. This is sometimes easy to forget, probably because the form is not solid. It often has empty spaces between the stems, leaves and flowers, and the separate parts, the leaves and petals, are usually flat.

However, a bunch of flowers, a potted plant or any other growing thing occupies space and therefore has a three-dimensional shape, albeit one with lots of gaps and spaces. You will get a better idea of this shape if you move around the subject and look at it from different angles.

To capture the three-dimensional form in a drawing or painting involves perspective. If a bunch of flowers is not to look like a flat shape, you have to convey the idea that some of the stems are leaning away from you and others towards you.

This is done partly by the perspective of the flower heads themselves: those leaning away are smaller and the shapes are interrupted by the nearer blooms. You can also convey the idea of space and distance by considering the perspective of the stems themselves. In other words, stems leaning away seem to get narrower as they taper into the distance; stems leaning towards you appear to get wider. In order not to end up with a flat image, avoid the tendency to depict all the stems in lines of equal width.

DRAWING

The following statement may seem obvious but it is very necessary: the first thing to do when making a drawing is to ensure that the subject will fit on to the paper or canvas. This first step, which will be explained below, is often neglected by beginners and it is surprising how many artists have problems with it.

You should also bear in mind that there is a distinct difference between making a drawing as a preparatory stage for a painting and making a drawing for its own sake. The second needs to have the quality of a finished work. Both types, however, must show the basic structure and proportions of the subject; and there are certain simple guidelines that make all drawing easier.

Positioning the subject

The best initial approach is to take one measurement from the subject and use this as a unit with which to measure everything else. Let us say, for example, that you are drawing a tulip in a pot. An obvious measurement here would be the height of the pot. Hold your pencil vertically, at arm's length, and align the top of the pencil with the top of the pot. Then move your thumb so that it marks the position of the bottom of the pot. This distance between your thumb and the top of the pencil is your basic measurement.

Still holding the pencil at arm's length, see how many times the pot's height fits into the subject (the tulip and the pot). Let us suppose, for example, that the pot fits twice into the height of the tulip. You are now able to mark the position of the top and bottom of the subject on the support, and then mark a third of the way up, to show where the top of the pot will be. In this way you can plot exactly where you want the subject to be within the composition.

Now, still taking the pot's height as your basic unit, use this to assess the size and position of everything else in the picture, indicating the position of each with a small mark. You can then continue with the drawing, using these fixed points as accurate guides.

◁ 1 *The artist starts by marking the position of the top and bottom of the jar on the paper. Using this measurement as a basic unit against which to measure the rest of the subject, the composition is then indicated with light pencil marks.*

▽ 2 *Using the marks as a guide, the composition is then developed as a light line drawing. In this case, the pencil lines are kept to a minimum so as not to interfere with ensuing colour.*

A finished drawing

The most popular drawing materials are graphite pencil and charcoal (there is more about the use of these materials on pages 76 and 78). However, crayon, pastel, coloured pencil and dip pens are among the many alternatives, and artists often work in a combination of two or more.

Whichever medium you choose, one of the most important factors is what we call quality of line. Lines should not only be accurate but also have a free, fluid quality, a flow that can capture the essence of the subject without necessarily including a lot of shading or detail.

This facility comes with experience and practice. Novices tend to be tense and often hold the drawing implement too tightly – usually too close to the drawing tip. Move your hand further back and loosen your grip, and you will find the tip moves with more freedom and gives you a more expressive line.

Drawing for painting

When drawing for a painting, whether this is in watercolours, oils or any other type of paint, the main purpose of the initial drawing is to provide a structure which will act as a guide for the ensuing colour. This guide may be very minimal, often no more than a skeleton of the subject. Or it may be a more detailed drawing in which specific areas of tone and texture are also indicated.

Again, charcoal and pencil are the most usual drawing materials, although some painters prefer to make their initial drawings with paint. Both charcoal and pencil can be rubbed back before starting to paint, so that the lines are not so obtrusive that they interfere with the finished work. A 'painted' drawing is usually absorbed and covered as work progresses.

◁ 3 *The finished painting is crisp and accurate, reflecting the care taken in the initial drawing stage.*

EXPLORING THE MEDIA

When you set out to paint flowers, you should not feel restricted to just one medium, such as only oils, only watercolour, or acrylic. As the opportunities occur, it is a good idea to explore the various materials covered in this book. Not only is it fun to try something new but each newly discovered medium will help you appreciate different aspects of the flowers and plants.

The works here use a wide variety of materials, including collage, charcoal and mixed media. The pictures differ enormously, and the varied approaches will help dispel the notion that flower paintings always have to be done in a certain way and on a small scale – small enough to 'suit the subject'. Some of the paintings, such as the pastel project on page 68, are tiny; but others, like the white lilies on page 52, are comparatively large.

Be creative

A collage is simply a picture built up from torn or cut-out paper, fabric and other scraps of material. It is not a technique with which to produce a realistic image, but it is a wonderful medium for expressing a subject in terms of texture, shape and colour, and it encourages you to think creatively using those elements.

Not only does collage produce exciting results in its own right; it also makes you see things in terms of the materials to hand. Thus, when you come to work in oils, watercolour or any other materials, you are less hampered by preconceived ideas and your appreciation of the subject is that much broader.

Oil ▽

△ Mixed media

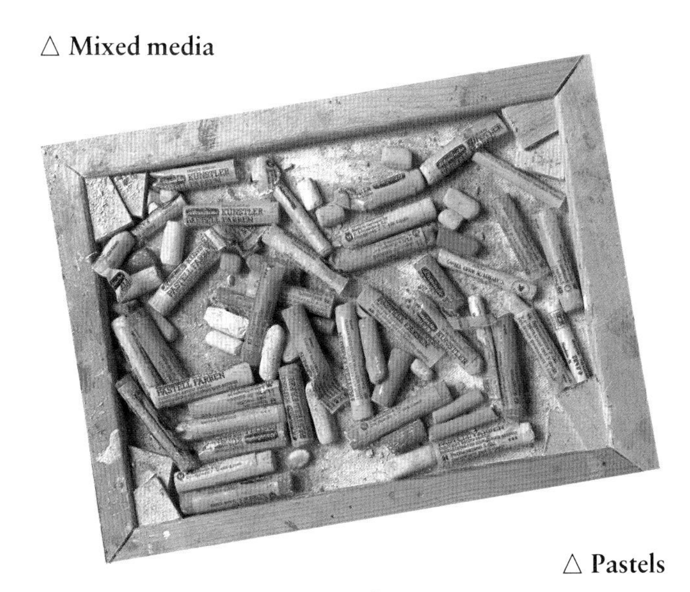

△ Pastels

Gouache ▷

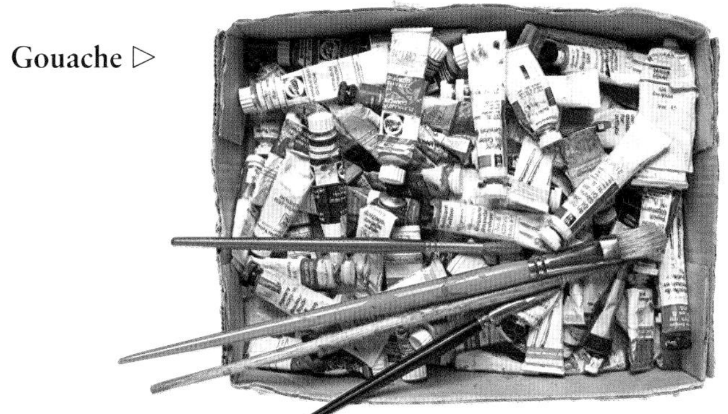

◁ Watercolour

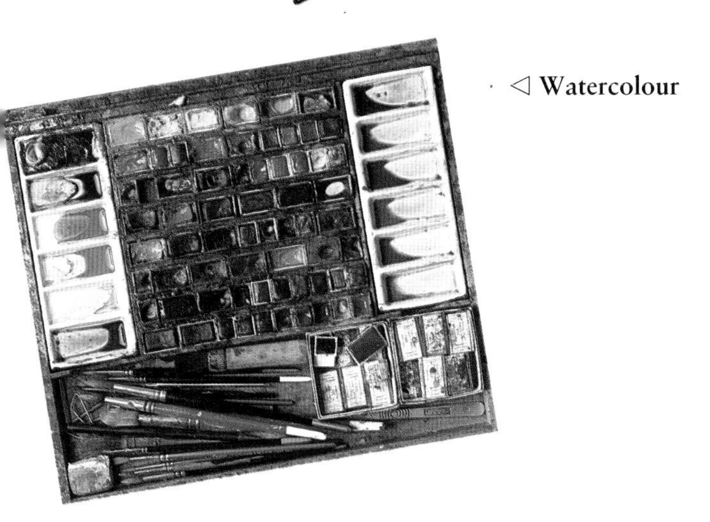

'Beginner's blight'

Charcoal and other chunky materials are also useful in that they enable you to get the subject established quickly and in general terms. The common tendency of starting work in a tight, inhibited manner is sometimes referred to as 'beginner's blight', but the problem is by no means confined to beginners. It is often suffered by experienced professional artists, and the remedy is always the same: you have to loosen up.

Any subject has to be simplified in the early stages of a painting, but flowers and plants call for particular caution. They have so much built-in detail that this can sometimes be difficult to ignore. The best way is to sidestep the problem by thinking 'big'. Choose a large piece of paper or canvas. Then start work with wide brushes, soft pencils or the chunkiest sticks of pastel or charcoal you can find – the sort used by scenic artists and signwriters is best because it comes in bigger sticks.

There is nothing to stop you developing the picture and bringing it up to quite a detailed, finished state. But the most important thing is to get the basics right first. Before anything else, the artist usually decides on the composition and blocks in the main areas of tone and colour. Only then is it time to start thinking about developing and tightening up specific areas.

Compatible materials

Whatever medium you are using, an open mind to both the materials and the subject will benefit the end result. With the exception of oils, which do not mix with water-based paints, the majority of art materials are compatible and can be used together in the same picture. Soft pastels, charcoal and chalk have to be fixed to stop them from smudging, but these too can be used with paints and other drawing materials.

The feathery nature of a pastel line is very different from the fine, precise quality of pen and ink. Watercolour washes are loose and transparent, compared with the solid opacity of gouache or acrylic. Every material has different characteristics, and there is absolutely no reason why some of these should not be combined in the same painting. So keep your options open. You are not necessarily confined to one medium.

COMPOSITION

Plan before you paint. Imagine that you have decided to paint a picture of a plant in a tub, on a garden bench. Do not jump straight in and start sketching the plant in its tub – that is, the subject – before you have decided where it should be positioned against the background. The garden and the bench may be subordinate, but they are nevertheless important. So think about the whole picture – the composition – before depicting the subject itself. The subject does not necessarily have to sit in the centre, although this may be what you want. The important thing is to decide beforehand.

If you do jump straight in and begin painting the plant in its tub, you will probably have missed the chance to achieve the most interesting composition; what is more, your subject might end up too small, leaving masses of unwanted surrounding space, or too large even to fit into the picture. Also, once you have committed yourself to paint, it is sometimes too late to change your composition.

Background has a shape

It is easy to think of a plant as a definite shape, but once you have drawn this on a rectangular sheet of paper or a canvas, you automatically create another shape: that of the background. When you go on to

Composition *These watercolour sketches show five possible approaches to the same subject. The artist has experimented not only with the scale and position of the subject within the picture, but has also varied the shape and proportion of each sketch.*

add the bench, you automatically create more surrounding shapes: the shapes left by the lines of the bench, plant and tub. These created shapes are just as important as the more obvious one of the main subject.

So, you should think, before you start, of the whole picture, comprising a set of interrelated shapes, background as well as subject. This will give you an overall arrangement or 'composition'.

Some possibilities

Sometimes you will choose an extremely straightforward subject, but even so you still have to think about the composition. The pictures on this page show the same simple subject arranged differently in the picture space. In all cases, note that the background spaces are important, whether or not the plant is in the centre. This applies both when the main subject is large and dominating and when it is a smaller element in the whole composition. The examples given here are only a small selection from an almost endless choice.

All these sketches are perfectly sound compositions and each is interesting in its own way. As you can see, the actual subject can be very small, with a lot of emphasis on the surrounding space, or it can fill up the entire picture area, with very little visible background. The important thing is to decide before you start just what you want, rather than leaving the composition to chance.

SKETCHING AND PLANNING

Sketching can be the key to planning your composition. Some artists make one large sketch, which can include more elements and areas than might eventually be used. This approach allows you to select and discard some of them.

A few simple devices can help you to view your rough drawing and explore different arrangements. You can cut a rectangular 'frame' from paper or a piece of card and place this on to the sketch, moving it around to show how the subject looks in different frameworks. A more flexible version of this is to cut out two L-shaped 'brackets' of card or paper. These can be moved closer together or further apart to give an idea of what the composition looks like in more squared or more elongated pictures. An additional option is to hold up your frame or L-shaped brackets in front of the actual subject itself, moving these around and altering the proportions of the rectangle until you find a shape to suit the subject.

Pencil is the most popular sketching tool. Some artists also use charcoal because of its facility for sketching rough tonal effects – dark and light shades – on to the paper, to see how painted tones might look in the composition. Watercolours or gouache can also be used for sketches to give some indication of how the colour might look in a finished picture.

The illustrations on this page show sample sketches and also examples of 'thumbnails'.

▽ **Sketchbooks** *Our artist carries one of these pocket-size sketchbooks around at all times, and finds them essential for on-the-spot sketching, making colour notes and recording ideas.*

◁ **Thumbnails** *Tiny colour sketches helped this artist work out the colours, tones and composition of the subject before starting work on the final painting.*

Thumbnail sketches

These are small rough drawings, quickly produced. Some artists spend only thirty seconds or so on each exploratory sketch, in order to get thoughts quickly on to paper so that choices can be made without spending too much time developing a particular approach. Speed also helps to achieve a spontaneous touch – although, of course, you can take as long as you wish. Thumbnail sketches are for your own use, so it does not matter how rough they are.

Take your paper or sketchbook and move round the subject, producing thumbnails from various different views. This will give you a choice of composition and also help you to understand the forms you are drawing.

Some artists find that the more quick sketches they produce in preparation for a painting, the more their ideas develop.

The rough sketches should not be thrown away when you have made your final drawing and moved to the painting stage. You can always return to them later for regeneration of ideas, and even dab colour on to them to experiment as you seek ways of developing the main painting.

CHAPTER 2 CHAPTER

Watercolour and gouache

FLOWERS ARE OFTEN transparent as well as colourful. Not only do their colours reflect the light, but the light shines through them. It is this translucent quality which makes flowers and plants such an attractive subject to the artist – while at the same time presenting the makers of paints with a challenging task. Probably the finest solution manufacturers have come up with is watercolours: their transparency is particularly well suited to capturing the brilliant, light-filtering colours of flowers and plants.

Traditional watercolours are available in pans and tubes. Gouache, also water-based but opaque instead of transparent, comes mainly in tubes and in strong colours which are good for the vividness needed in some approaches to flower painting.

Usually soft brushes are used for both watercolour and gouache. The traditional sable and other natural-hair brushes are preferred by many because of their strong, pliant bristles and their capacity for holding a lot of colour. However, there are now many excellent soft synthetic brushes on the market.

◁ **Watercolour** *The transparency of the medium allowed the artist, David Hutter, to exploit the whiteness of the paper in this painting. Layers of transparent yellow laid over bright white paper give the painted image the translucent quality of a rose.*

△ **Gouache, watercolour and ink** *In this mixed-media work, the wild flowers are central to what is otherwise a landscape. The artist, Sally Michel, has painted flowers in their natural setting to give texture and colour to a rural scene.*

TECHNIQUES

WET AND DRY EFFECTS

Watercolour is probably the favourite medium for flower painting, as it is extremely flexible. You can paint very precisely or you can achieve loose, washy effects, depending on how you apply the colour.

Both these approaches are useful for flower painting, because you will sometimes want to capture the amorphous effects of colours running together – perhaps in the background, or to create the mottled texture of particular leaves and petals – and yet, in the same painting, you may also want to depict certain precise details.

Painting on to wet colour gives a loose, runny effect; painting on to dry colour produces crisply defined edges. You can use both techniques in the same painting.

An image which is tightly painted all over can look much less interesting and effective than one which contains detail only in selected areas. For instance, you might paint the flower heads quite loosely, allowing the colours to run into each other in a random way, and then allow this to dry before painting the centre of the flowers with a small brush in a sharply defined manner.

The defined flower centres will draw the viewer's eye and bring the rest of the painting – the blurred flower heads – into focus.

Wet on wet

Colours run if you paint on to wet paper or an area of wet colour. The effects can be stunning, but to

▽ **Wet on dry** *When wet paint is applied over a dry colour, the image is crisp and sharply defined.*

some extent the result is random, because you can never have absolute control, especially if the first colour is very wet. However, if you allow the first colour partially to dry, until it is damp rather than soaking wet, then a second colour can be applied with more confidence. Your second colour will keep its approximate shape, running just enough to give it a soft, blurred edge.

It is worth practising the 'wet-on-wet' technique to find out what results you get by painting on to paper of varying degrees of wetness.

Wet on dry

Botanical painters tend to use watercolour simply because it can be so accurate. But to be used with precision, each colour must be allowed to dry before the next is added. If you are using one colour next to, or on top of, another, the first must be absolutely dry; otherwise they will both run.

When you apply watercolour to a dry surface, whether this is white paper or an area of painted colour, the new colour retains the shape of the brushstroke. If you drag the loaded brush smoothly across the paper, you will get a regular, even edge to the painted shape. If you apply the colour in jerky strokes, then you will get a correspondingly jagged outline. By painting wet on dry, you will retain the shape of each brushstroke exactly as it is applied to the paper.

Watercolour brushes and papers come in a wide range of sizes, so the 'wet-on-dry' approach works on any scale. A large wash brush can cover big areas very quickly; the smallest sable brush will paint the finest line or tiniest dot. Working in this way, you will always have absolute control over what you are doing.

You do, however, need to be patient. The wet paint can take some time to dry, especially if it is diluted with a lot of water. A hairdryer can speed up this process so long as you use it carefully.

▽ **Wet on wet** *A soft amorphous quality is the result of applying paint to colour that is still damp.*

TECHNIQUES

TRANSPARENT AND OPAQUE

There are two distinct types of watercolour paint, those which are opaque and those which have a transparent quality. Classical watercolours are virtually transparent, but gouache contains chalk or a similar filler, which makes the colours solid and opaque. Although watercolour and gouache are often lumped together because they are both technically watercolour paints, the two products are actually very different and therefore call for very different approaches.

To get some idea of this, look at the two paintings below. The same subject is painted first in traditional watercolour and then in opaque gouache. The watercolour is characteristically transparent, producing a light, shimmering effect; the gouache, on the other hand, is bold and bright, capturing different aspects and giving a contrasting impression of the subject.

Transparent watercolour

Perhaps there is no manufactured medium that can truly capture the effect of sunlight behind a brilliantly coloured flower. But of all the materials available to us, watercolour is certainly the one that comes closest to achieving this. For this reason it has been a favourite of flower painters for generations, and each colour of nature has a very near equivalent on the watercolourist's palette.

Classical watercolour painting is carried out by building up layers of thin colour on white paper. Because the paints are transparent, it is necessary to lay the paler colours first and then build up the

△ **Watercolour white** *In this watercolour the white paper is used to represent the flowers. The background is painted around each shape, and shadows are painted on.*

image gradually with increasingly dark layers of colour. This technique, often referred to as working 'light to dark' means any white areas and highlights are left as areas of white paper, so you have to decide in advance where these areas are going to be.

For flower painters, the great advantage of this 'layer-by-layer' approach is that you can get the translucent and amorphous effects of natural colour in a way that is impossible with opaque colour. Look at the reds and yellows in the tulip painting on page 36. The colours seem glowing and natural simply because the yellow underpainting gleams through the red to produce an uneven effect, ranging from rich crimson to deep orange – exactly like the real flower.

With overlaid watercolour, the colours underneath can be seen through the top layers, depending on how thick or dark the paint is. By overlaying the watercolour in this way, you not only re-create the variegated or mottled colour of many flowers, leaves and petals but also retain the transparent quality of the subject.

Opaque paints

Gouache colours are solid and opaque. They are popular with many flower artists for their bold, brilliant colours and for the lively, spontaneous images they are able to produce. As you can see from the project on pages 44 and 45, gouache colours can also be heavily diluted with water to produce a washy effect that is almost transparent, although never with the fineness and translucency of true watercolour.

Unlike watercolour, gouache has a strong covering capacity. In other words, you can paint a light colour over a darker one and cover it easily, provided the paint has not been too diluted. Mistakes can be instantly obliterated, and colours and tones quickly corrected. These qualities make gouache an ideal sketching medium – good for on-the-spot painting and for bold, spontaneous colour work.

△ **Opaque white** *White gouache is opaque and can be used on top of a deeper colour. The white petal highlights are painted in gouache over a darker colour.*

TECHNIQUES

WHITES AND LIGHTS

We know that watercolour painters avoid using white paint with other colours because it makes the colours look chalky and they lose their characteristic transparency. We know too that the whites in a watercolour painting should be patches of white paper, and that pale shades are created by adding varying amounts of water to the different colours.

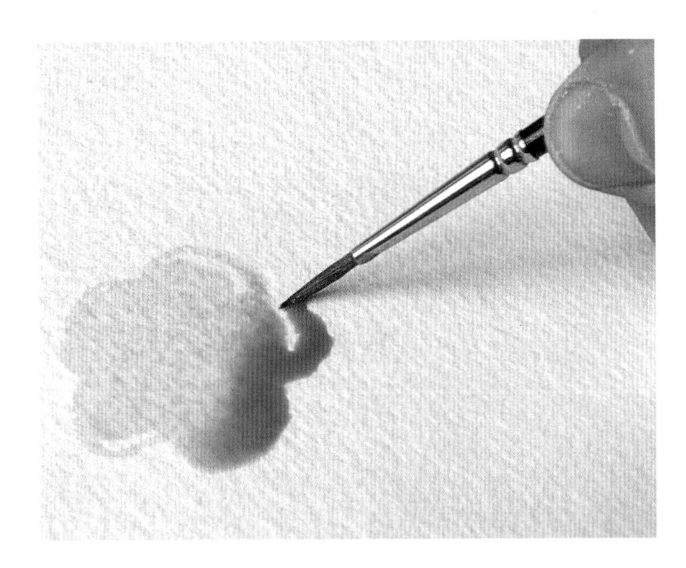

Obviously, however, theory is one thing and reality another, and if you forget to leave a white highlight, then the sensible solution is to go over it with a blob of white paint. With gouache there is never a problem, because the whites can be added at the last minute – which makes it all very much easier.

If possible, plan your whites when using watercolour, so that you know which areas of paper to leave blank. Use white paint only if really necessary and in a limited way. This may seem like splitting hairs; after all, white is white, and does it really matter how you get it? But there is a distinct difference in quality between the white of the paper and the white that has been painted in later. The demonstrations below show two paintings of the same flower. In the first, the white highlight is represented by the white of the paper, and the effect is truly that of a transparent watercolour. The second shows the highlight painted in opaque white gouache – an altogether stronger image.

Watercolour white

◁ △ **1** *The palest tones are laid leaving patches of white paper to represent the white tones and highlights.*

◁ **2** *When the first wash is dry, the artist applies a slightly darker colour, the middle tone. Patches of the underlying pale wash are allowed to show through to represent the palest tones on the petals. The white highlights are left untouched.*

△ **3** *In the finished flower, white highlights, pale tones and shadows – depicted in that order – describe the shape and form of the subject.*

For a strong as opposed to a translucent image, use gouache rather than watercolour from the start. With the opaque gouache, the whites and lights are no different from the brighter and darker colours, and can be applied as you work.

Other whites

For small areas, particularly details such as flower centres, tiny dots of white paint are effective and do not interfere with an otherwise transparent image. It is also possible to scratch back into the paint to reveal the white paper underneath – again, this is strictly for creating small flecks and detail, but these can be very effective in enlivening an otherwise flat or dull area of colour.

Correcting mistakes

On small areas, if you accidentally paint something too dark or use the wrong colour, quickly flood the area with clean water. Squeeze any excess moisture from the brush and lift as much colour as possible from the support before the paint starts to dry.

Major mistakes in watercolour painting are more difficult to deal with, especially if the paint has already dried. There is no really effective way of lightening or removing a large area of watercolour. Sometimes household bleach applied with a cotton bud is effective, but this is not suitable if you want a completely even result. In addition, some pigments are very strong and can survive several applications of neat bleach.

The best way of avoiding mistakes is to test each tone and colour before applying it to the picture. Once you start doing this, it quickly becomes a habit, and saves time and disappointment in the long run. It also gives you much greater control over the work.

Opaque white

△ 1 *For the palest tone, the artist applies a diluted wash over the entire flower.*

▷ △ 2 *A second tone, a slightly darker wash, is then laid over the dry light tones. Patches of the lighter tone are allowed to show through the deeper colour, and opaque gouache added for the white highlights and yellow centre.*

▷ 3 *The opaque white is brighter than the white of the paper, and the highlights stand out starkly. Each painted highlight shape retains the shape of the brushstroke – a much stronger effect than the watercolour whites shown opposite.*

TECHNIQUES

MASKING

Artists often avoid painting flowers in their own natural environment simply because masses of them grow together! While painting a single daisy or even a vase of daisies may seem a feasible proposition, painting a whole field of them is a different matter altogether.

With watercolour this is even more of a problem: as the paint is transparent, this rules out the possibility of painting the flower heads on top of the grass, which is a darker tone. There are basically two ways to proceed. You can, of course, use a more opaque paint, such as gouache, poster colour or acrylic, for the paler flower heads. All of these are capable of covering a darker colour, provided you use them thickly enough.

The alternative is to use masking fluid, as the artist does here and in the project painting on page 38, where the painter tackles a branch of white blossom.

Masking fluid

This liquid rubbery solution can be painted on to those areas of the paper which need to be left white – in this case, the daisies. When the fluid is dry,

△ 1 *Masking fluid is applied to those areas to be protected from the paint and then allowed to dry.*

△ 2 *Paint can now be safely applied around and over the masked areas. Here the artist paints the yellow centres of the daisies.*

◁ 3 *Background foliage is added. This is taken up to and over the edges of the masked petals.*

these areas can be painted over quite safely without the colour affecting the paper underneath.

Masking fluid is available from art shops, and is usually either pale yellow or colourless. The advantage of the coloured fluid is that it can be seen quite clearly against a white paper, so you can see exactly where your masked areas are. All masking fluids will ruin a good paint brush, however quickly or thoroughly you clean it after use, so keep an old one specially for the purpose.

When the masking fluid is dry, the rubbery skin is rubbed away from the masked areas to reveal the crisp white shapes underneath. You can remove the mask with an eraser or your finger; both of them must be scrupulously clean to avoid dirt becoming ingrained in the paper. Rub carefully to prevent the paper surface from coming away with the mask.

Masking fluid is best suited to small areas, and in any case is less necessary for large shapes, which can simply be painted around. On a large scale it can be unwieldy and messy to remove.

When revealed, the white masked areas have hard edges and will probably stand out starkly in the painting, rather like cut-out shapes. This may be what you want, but if not you can counteract the effect by muting the white shapes with a pale, neutral wash or by suggesting petal shapes and shadows – as the artist does here.

Other masking techniques

For a more textural effect, use wax crayons or even a domestic candle for masking. These can be scribbled over a whole area to get a broken texture, or you can use them to create soft pastel-like lines.

Obviously a wax crayon is coloured, and the colour will become part of the painting. A domestic candle, on the other hand, has no colour and is virtually transparent when used in this way, so it allows the colour of the paper to show through.

Alternatives to masking

For the odd detail you will probably find masking of any sort unnecessary. A touch of white gouache will suffice for a tiny white stamen or a few white speckles on a coloured petal. If you are careful, you can even scratch into the dried paint with a sharp scalpel to reveal the paper underneath, although this is effective only if used in a limited way and on a very small area.

△ ◁ 4 *When the paint is dry, the rubbery mask can be removed by rubbing with a clean finger or soft eraser.*

◁ 5 *The revealed white petal shapes are crisp and clean, retaining the shape of the brushstrokes used to apply the masking fluid.*

TECHNIQUES

TEXTURE AND COLOUR

Patterns and textures are everywhere, and for the artist this can be both a challenge and a delight. The first thing to bear in mind is that textures often look more important than they really are and can be confusing for this reason. A patterned leaf, coarse tree bark, a flecked petal – all have pronounced surface qualities that tend to jump out and take our attention away from the rest of the subject. Surface textures and patterns can therefore disguise the form and structure of the subject and can often be overemphasized in the painting.

Say, for instance, you are painting a potted plant which has unusual variegated leaves. You immediately notice and start worrying about the mottled leaves because they are more visually prominent than anything else. The more striking the pattern, the more difficult it can be actually to see the form of the leaf, because the pattern makes it more difficult to see areas of light and shade.

The secret is to be selective about texture and pattern and not let them dominate the whole picture. It is always a good idea to look at the

Texture with gum arabic

▽ 1 *Working in watercolour, the artist first applies a flat yellow to the leaf shapes and allows this to dry.*

▽▽ 2 *Leaf green is mixed with a little gum arabic before being painted over the yellow shapes.*

△△ 3 *Gum arabic gives watercolour a viscous texture, which then dries with a slightly glossy finish.*

△ 4 *When the paint-and-gum-arabic colour is dry, clean water is spattered across the painted surface.*

subject through half-closed eyes. The blurred image that you see will obliterate detail and surface effects and you can more easily pick out the basic structure and form.

Spattering

One of the most useful texture-making techniques for the flower painter is spattering. It creates a delightful speckled or mottled texture that can be applied sparsely or densely as the subject requires. Spattering is done simply by dipping the tips of the paintbrush bristles in paint and flicking the colour across the required area. You can use either watercolour or gouache, working with very diluted paint for a pale, barely discernible effect or thicker colour if you want a stronger contrast.

Spattering with gum arabic

In the demonstration below the artist is using gum arabic to capture the subtle, spattered texture of a variegated laurel leaf. Gum arabic is normally mixed with paint to give lustre to the dried colour. In this case, it is mixed with the paint to make the colour more soluble.

The artist painted a flat pale green over the leaf shape, waited till this was dry, then overpainted with a darker green mixed with a little gum arabic. Once dry, the dark green was spattered lightly with water, which dissolved the dark-green and gum-arabic mixture. The droplets of water were then immediately blotted off to reveal the light green underneath.

◁ 5 *The spattered water dissolves the paint and gum arabic, which can then be blotted off with tissue.*

△ 6 *Here a spattered effect has been used to create the texture of a spotted laurel leaf, but you can apply water in different ways to create many other effects.*

PROJECTS

TULIP

Watercolour

Watercolour at its simplest and most effective. The tulip is naturalistic and detailed but, contrary to appearances, the picture took less than an hour to paint – much of this waiting for the paint to dry in between stages. Although both drawing and painting were kept to a minimum, the accuracy of the initial pencil drawing was crucial. A fine outline with a B pencil was a precise guide for the subsequent layers of colour: sap green, cadmium yellow and alizarin crimson, with Payne's grey and cobalt blue for the darker tones.

Classical approach

Flower and foliage are painted in the classical manner from light to dark. Three tones of green are used for the leaves: light, medium and dark. The petals are painted in three tones of yellow, with the alizarin crimson markings added last.

The light-to-dark approach is seen clearly here in the leaves. A very light wash is applied on the whole leaf. When this dries, the artist applies the medium tone, leaving the pale highlights. Finally, the darkest areas are added to the shaded parts.

This picture is mostly painted on to dry colour. The artist waited for each layer to dry before applying the next. Occasionally, this approach was deliberately interrupted and the artist painted on to a damp patch of colour. Again, these looser areas can be seen clearly on the leaves. Use of a hairdryer speeded up the drying between stages.

The background

In the interest of clarity, the background here is left unpainted, without even a shadow to indicate a feeling of space around the tulip. This absolute plainness is unusual in paintings, because an unpainted background is inevitably seen as a flat, two-dimensional plane, whereas the subject is obviously intended to look three-dimensional.

△ 1 *Before starting to paint, the artist draws the outline of the tulip lightly but precisely with a 2B pencil. A very diluted wash of cadmium yellow is applied across the whole of the flower, followed by a similarly weak wash of sap green on the leaf and stem. Both these colours are then allowed to dry.*

△ 2 *The lightest areas of the leaves are left in the initial pale green as the artist overpaints a slightly stronger green tone across the rest of the leaves and stem. A touch of Payne's grey and cobalt blue is added to this second tone in order to darken the colour.*

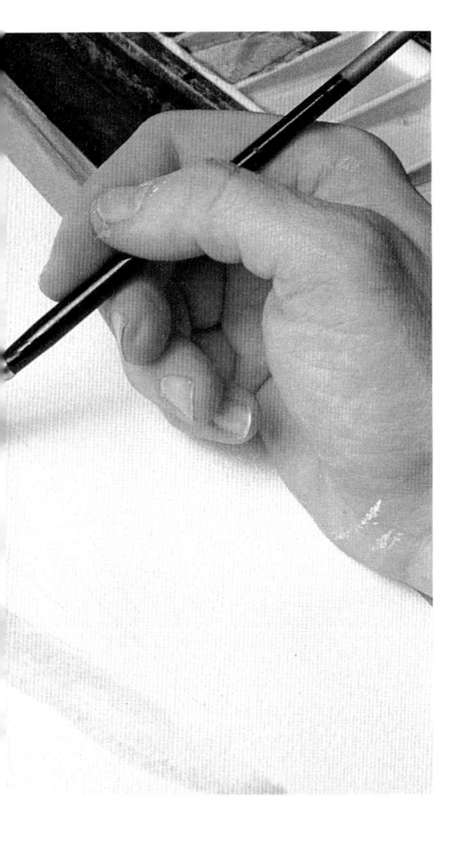

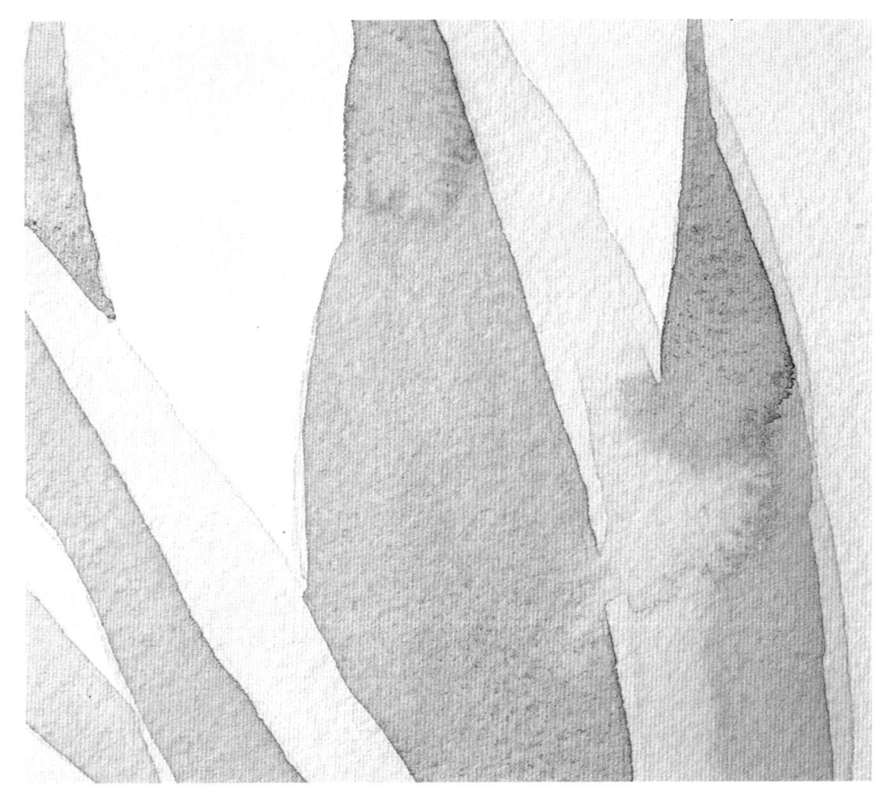

△▷ 3 *The whole painting is generally worked 'wet on dry'. However, in certain places the artist dampens the underlying colour to allow the second layer of overlaid paint to run slightly. Here the rather regular lines of the leaves are deliberately broken by causing the light and mid-greens to run and merge in certain, limited areas.*

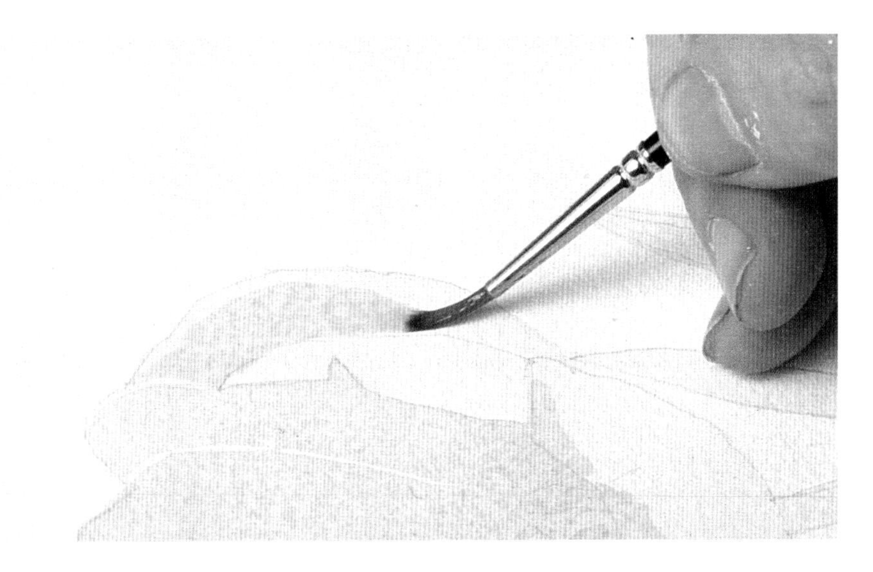

▷ 4 *The yellow tulip heads are treated in a similar way. A darker yellow is applied to all but the very palest areas of the petals.*

◁ 5 *Tiny flecks of the initial pale wash show through the second layer of yellow. These represent the delicate pale highlights on the curved ends of the petals. Even at this stage, the subject has a three-dimensional quality, as these initial, carefully observed tones already begin to indicate the forms of the flower and leaves.*

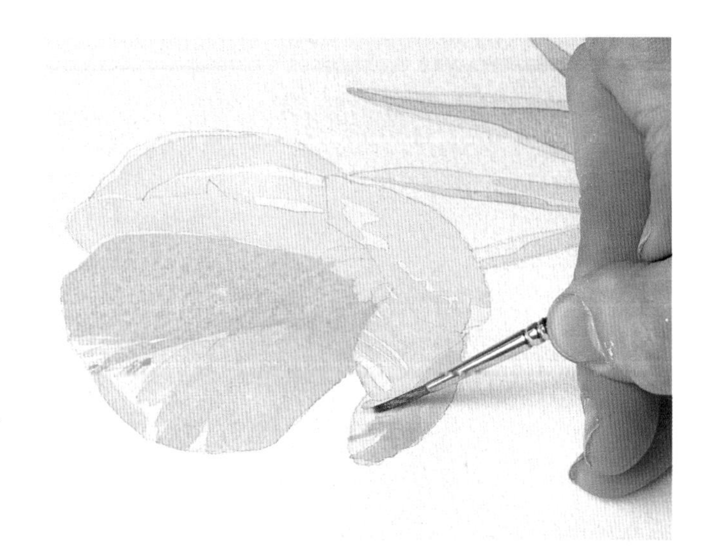

▷ **6** *The final, deepest yellow is now applied to the shaded areas of the tulip. This darker tone is achieved by adding more paint to the previous diluted colour.*

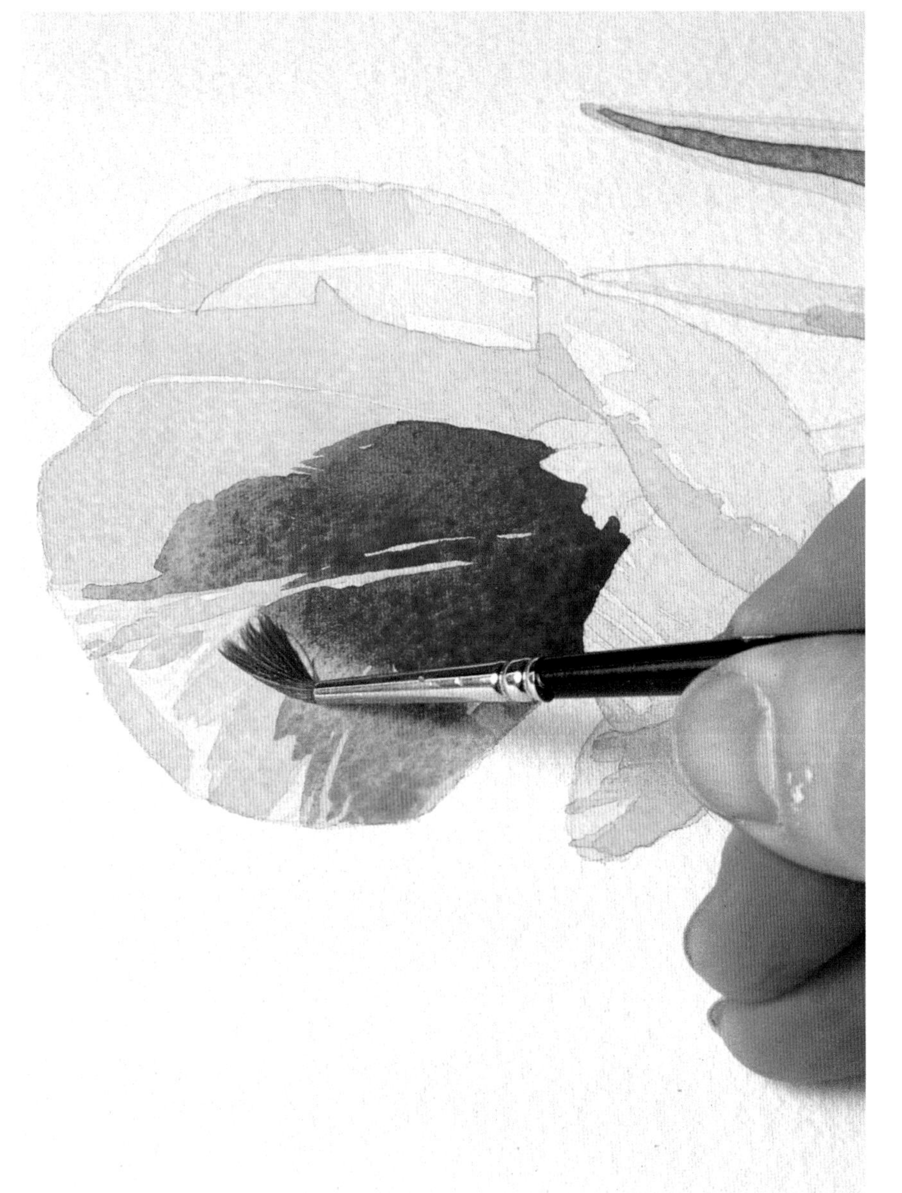

◁ 7 *After painting the alizarin crimson centre, the artist spreads the colour into the surrounding yellow, diluting the edges of the red shape with water so that it merges into the rest of the flower.*

▷ **8** *The red of the outer petals is added in a similar manner. The deeper inside tones are darkened with a little Payne's grey, applied 'wet on wet'.*

▷ **9** *Tiny coloured ridges, barely visible on the subject, are painted with diluted alizarin and applied with the tip of a fine sable brush.*

▽ **10** *The head of the tulip is now finished. With just two main colours – cadmium yellow and alizarin – the artist has successfully described the local colour, the three-dimensional structure and the surface patterns of the flower.*

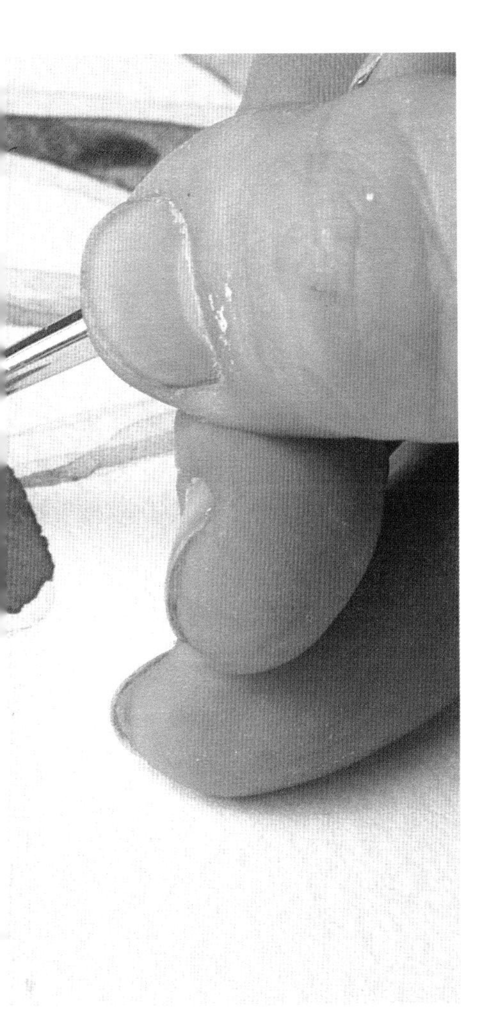

△ **11** *Sap green mixed with Payne's grey is used for the darkest shadow areas on the leaves.*

◁ **12** *The finished painting is simple in the extreme. The leaves are basically sap green; the flower, red and yellow. Yet by limiting the local colour of the subject to three tones, the artist has achieved an absolutely naturalistic image. The secret here lies in the precision of the initial drawing and the unfussy, yet accurate, application of colour.*

PROJECTS

PLUM BLOSSOM

Watercolour

A complicated subject can often be approached in a very simple way. Usually, the simpler the technique, the more effective the result.

Masking fluid

The prospect of painting this mass of tiny white blossoms against a darker background could have been daunting for any watercolour painter. Yet this artist did not take the obvious step of painting the flowers with opaque white paint. Nor did he attempt the time-consuming alternative of painting the background around each blossom.

He decided instead to use masking fluid. This enabled him to mask out and protect the white blossom shapes before attempting to paint the background. The sky was then blocked in by taking the colour across the masked shapes.

Space and perspective

Branches and twigs radiate outwards, usually from a main stem, tapering away from the growth points. The artist was able to achieve this effect by using a pointed sable brush. As the twig tapered, he narrowed the painted line by gradually decreasing the amount of pressure on the brush.

In this case the branches are dark and matt, and there is no obvious source of strong light. This meant there was no visible light and shade on the twigs to indicate the rounded form of each one. This, in turn, made it difficult to see whether a particular twig passed in front of or behind another.

The lack of obvious form made it especially important to avoid making the branch look like a flat shape. The artist therefore had to rely on the tapering technique, not only to make each twig taper in a natural way but also to give the branch a sense of space and perspective. In other words, the branches pointing towards the artist appeared to taper less than those pointing outwards, away from the artist.

△ 1 *The first stage of this painting is a line drawing, showing clearly the position and shape of the branches, leaves and blossoms. The artist then applies masking fluid to each of the white blossoms.*

▽ 2 *When the masking fluid is dry, the branches are painted with a fine sable brush in a mixture of Payne's grey and yellow ochre.*

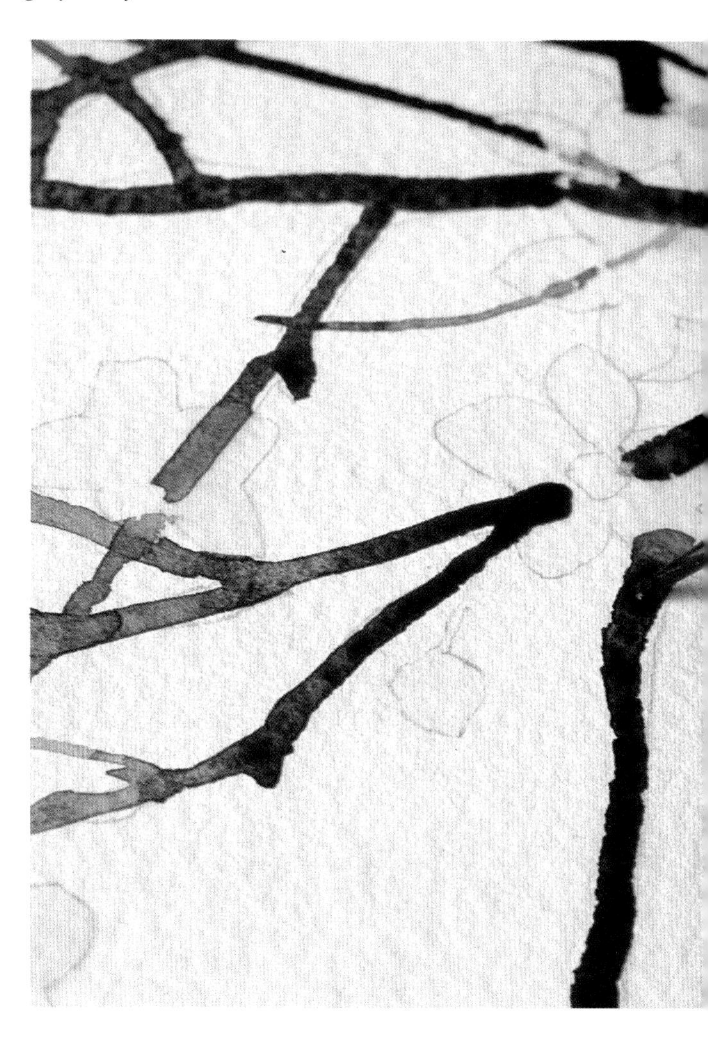

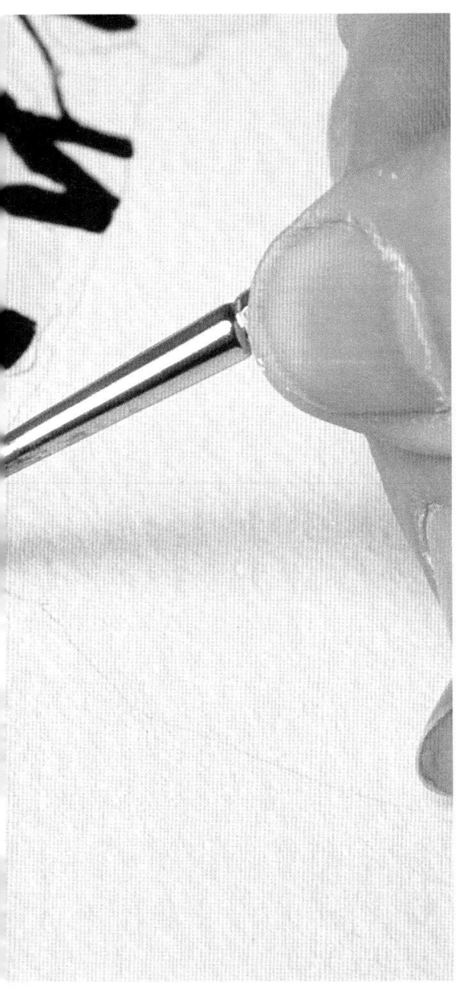

△ 3 *The pointed sable brush helped the artist vary the thickness of the branch and twigs by increasing or decreasing pressure to obtain a thicker or thinner line. To vary the tones within the branches, blobs of darker colour were added in certain areas and allowed to flood into the wet paint. The fine point of the brush was used for the tapering, growing tips of the twigs.*

▽ 4 *Leaves are painted in sap green with a touch of Payne's grey. A little gum arabic is added to thicken the paint and to give the leaves a slight gloss.*

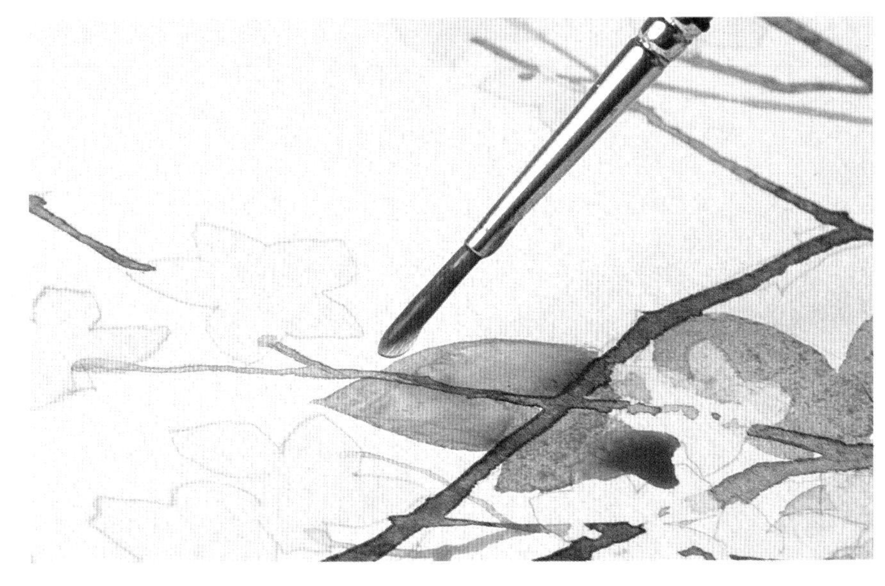

△ **5** *Although the leaves are painted in flat green, with no consciously observed lighter or darker tones, the paint is applied liberally. The artist then tilts the board slightly, causing reservoirs of colour to gather at the lower edges of the leaves. These dry as areas of dark tone, giving the impression of natural-looking shadows.*

▷ **6** *The pot is painted with a light wash of cobalt blue and yellow ochre, and a thin strip of darker colour is painted down the shadow side of the pot. The neck of the pot is painted in Payne's grey, with a darker blob of tone to indicate the shadow.*

▽ 7 *A diluted mixture of cobalt blue and brown madder alizarin is painted on to the background. This is taken right up to and over the masked blossoms.*

△ 8 *The background has been painted around the branches – time-consuming, but the artist wanted to retain the crisp, angular shapes of the branches and this was the best way to do so.*

△ **9** *Each masked shape is carefully rubbed out. It is advisable to rub briskly and lightly; if you are too vigorous the surface of the paper will come off with the mask.*

△▷ **10** *The blossoms are revealed as clear shapes against the darker background, and are now ready for further development.*

▷ **11** *Each flower centre is painted in a mixture of yellow ochre and cobalt blue.*

◁ **12** *The tiny shadow areas visible between some of the petals are picked out in a diluted mixture of cobalt blue and brown madder alizarin. The details of the flower centres are dotted in, using a darker version of the same colour.*

▽ **13** *The effectiveness of the completed painting lies in its absolute simplicity. The drawing and painting were both kept to a minimum, and the artist chose a limited palette of black, sap green, Payne's grey, cobalt blue, yellow ochre and brown madder alizarin. Apart from the masking fluid, a little gum arabic was used on the leaves.*

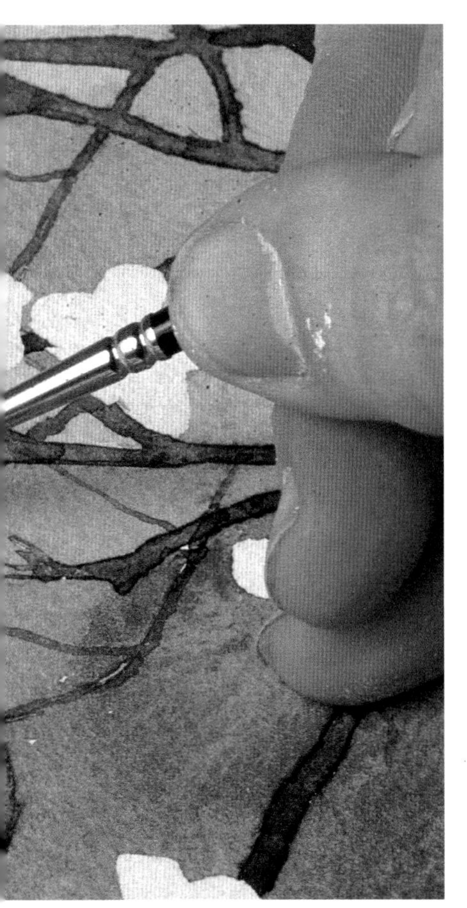

PROJECTS

ANEMONES

▽ 1 *Working on a sheet of grey sugar paper, the artist starts by blocking in some of the main areas of colour. No preliminary drawing was done for this painting.*

Gouache

Sunlit anemones in a green vase provide a colourful subject for this gouache painting. The opaque paints gave the artist plenty of scope to depict the flowers as lively splashes of colour and also to emphasize the light with bold strokes of solid white and yellow.

An immediate medium

The approach here is the opposite of that employed in the previous two projects, both of which were done in watercolour. With watercolour, the painting must normally be planned and worked out carefully, because each stroke becomes part of the finished picture. Gouache has very different qualities.

There was not even a preliminary drawing here. The artist plunged straight in with colour, starting with the vase and a few of the flowers. Broad brushstrokes suggest the approximate shape of each flower head, and the vase is blocked in with a confident bright green.

Although gouache is essentially opaque, it can be diluted with water to obtain a semi-transparent effect. In this painting the artist uses both solid and diluted colour. This was done partly in order to vary the paint texture and partly in order to indicate the different qualities within the subject.

Toned papers

Unlike watercolour, gouache can be used on toned and even brightly coloured papers. Here the artist chose a light, neutral grey to contrast with the vivid colours used in the painting.

Although many of the toned papers available in art shops are thick and of good quality, heavy wetting will usually cause them to buckle. In this painting, most of the background area was left untouched and stretching was therefore unnecessary. Generally, however, you would be well advised either to stretch the paper before painting or, alternatively, to mount it on a stiff sheet of card.

▷ 2 *The subject is now established within the picture area, and the artist is able to add the remaining blooms and to strengthen and redefine the earlier blocked-in shapes.*

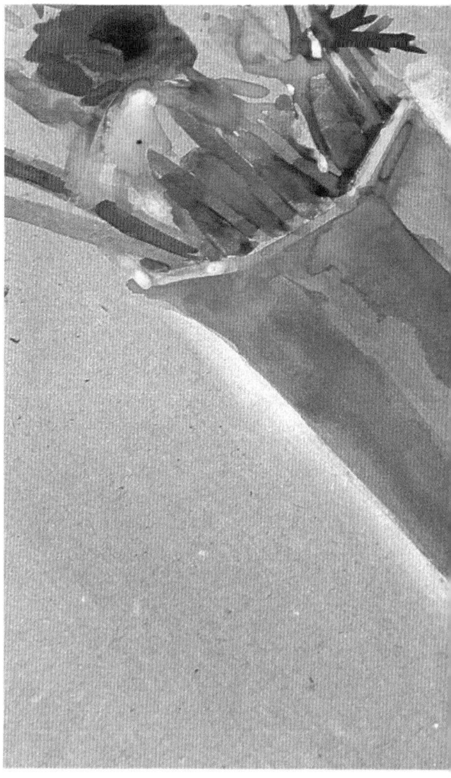

◁ 3 *Loose shadows of black and dark green are added to the vase. The background area is suggested in washy tones of medium yellow and black.*

▽ 4 The vase is completed with a deep-green shadow and a white highlight around the rim. Opaque white with yellow is applied boldly to the background and tabletop to indicate strong sunlight.

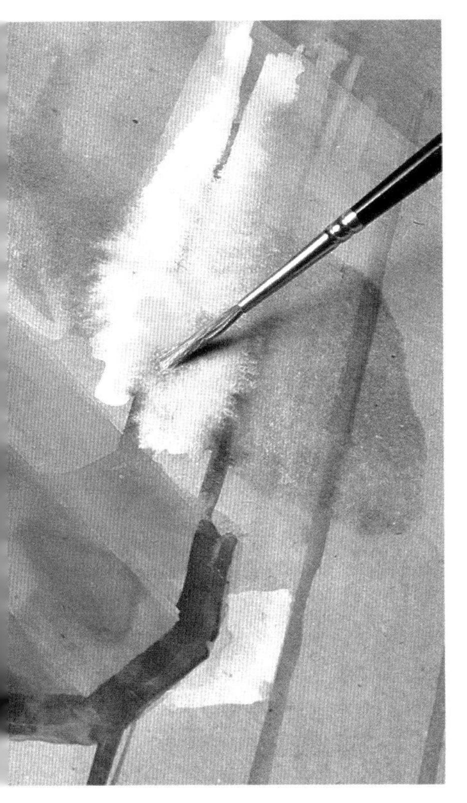

▷ 5 Finally, the checked tablecloth is lightly sketched in with paint. Colour is the most important element in this painting, and the artist captures the vivid hues of the subject by using some of the brightest pigments in the gouache range. The unmixed colours and lively, rapid approach give this finished painting the freshness and spontaneity of a colour sketch.

CHAPTER 3 CHAPTER

Oils and acrylic

BOTH THESE MEDIA allow for a lot of opportunity to move and manipulate the paint once it is on the canvas. You can make radical corrections simply by painting over what you have already done.

Oil paints are diluted with turpentine or spirit, and acrylics with water. Both are versatile. They can be used for fine development and also for a more rapid, bolder rendering of the subject. Initially, if you are unfamiliar with the media, you would be well advised to stick to a broader treatment, and so we have asked our artists here to bear this in mind.

Although oils and acrylic look similar and have a similar texture as they are squeezed on to the palette, there is one very important difference: drying times. Acrylics dry quickly: a thin layer of paint can dry within minutes. Oils take far longer, especially if you use the paint thickly; in that case the surface can become unworkable and you may have to put the work aside for a day or two before continuing. With acrylics the advantage is that you can block in areas of colour and paint quickly; with slower-drying oils, the advantage is that the paint remains malleable on the canvas for much longer.

Colour and texture *Oils and acrylics are versatile paints. They can be applied as thin washes, to create layers of transparent colour; or thickly, to achieve a richly textured paint surface. In this oil painting by Jack Millar, various brushstrokes are employed to describe the many contrasting textures within the subject.*

IMPASTO AND GLAZING

Thickly applied paint is known as 'impasto' and layers of thin overlaid colour are referred to as 'glazing'. These techniques can be used separately or you can combine the two by glazing layers of thin colour over an area of thick paint.

Painted texture

The great advantage of the impasto technique is that textures can actually be introduced into the paint itself, giving the work an almost three-dimensional quality. Thus if there are pronounced directional ridges in the petals or stems, for instance, these can be suggested by the direction of the painted brushstrokes. You can literally use the thick paint to describe the direction, form and shape of the subject.

The impastoed chrysanthemum below has an almost sculptured appearance, as the artist builds up thicker and thicker layers of paint to describe the tightly folded petals of the flower head.

You can also use impastoed paint to give a sense of space and perspective. An arrangement of cut flowers, for example, can be made to look three-dimensional simply by painting the blooms and stalks in the foreground on top of those which are further away, and by painting the foreground flowers with thicker and bigger brushstrokes.

Transparent glazes

The colours of nature are inevitably more luminous

Impasto

◁ ◁ 1 *The artist starts by blocking in the main shape of the chrysanthemum in fairly thin orange paint. This orange represents the darkest tones within the flower.*

◁ 2 *The tightly folded petals are then painted in thicker, less diluted colour. The rounded brushstrokes describe exactly the curved form of the petals, which are depicted here in paler tones of orange and yellow.*

◁ ◁ 3 *Finally, undiluted paint is used to add the lightest tones and highlights. Again, each petal is described by a single, curved brushstroke.*

◁ 4 *The paint here is thick enough to retain the texture and form of the petals, giving the chrysanthemum an almost three-dimensional quality. Acrylic paint was used for this demonstration; oils would have produced a similar effect, although they would have taken longer to dry.*

and transparent than the colours on your palette allow you to mix, and paint can seem a clumsy and inadequate means of reproducing the colours of flowers and foliage.

The answer is to apply the colour in glazes rather than solid strokes. Lay thin layers of paint over each other, and the underlying colours can be seen through. Thus you can obtain a more luminous orange by glazing yellow over red than by mixing the two colours together on the palette first, in which case the resulting orange will be solid and opaque.

Oil or acrylic?

Impasto and glazing can be done with oil or acrylic.

Originally impasto was an oil-painting technique, and in the past the disadvantage has always been the slow-drying nature of the paint – the thicker you used it, the longer it took to dry. Nowadays, however, there are special media to speed up the drying time of the paints, as well as a proprietary 'brushmark' gel, a thick medium that helps the paint retain the shape and texture of the brushstrokes.

Acrylic paints are relatively fast-drying, which makes them ideally suited to impasto painting. You can use either a brush or a painting knife to apply colour, depending on the effect you want. With a brush the paint surface retains the characteristic marks of brushstrokes and bristle marks. A knife is ideal for laying flat wedges of thick colour.

Similarly, you can glaze with both oils and acrylics, but the transparency and translucency of the colour will be improved if you mix the paint with one of the special glazing media available. Remember, oil and acrylic paints are not compatible, so you will need the appropriate medium for the type of paint you are working with.

Glazing

△ 1 *An ivy leaf is painted with thin colour to show broad areas of shadow and reflection.*

▷ △ 2 *The artist wanted to add richer tones to the leaf without obliterating the established form. This is done with a glaze of dark-green paint mixed with glazing medium.*

▷ 3 *Glazing gives the leaf a glossy, translucent finish, very similar to that of the actual ivy leaf. For the purpose of this demonstration, the artist chose quick-drying acrylics. Oils would have produced a similar result.*

PROJECTS

WHITE LILIES

Oils

These lilies, placed against a striking red backcloth, have a dynamic quality that the artist was anxious to capture in the painting. The attraction of the subject was the explosive appearance of the arrangement as a whole. This, the artist felt, was far more important than the intricate structure of the individual flowers.

Oil paint provided the perfect medium for this subject. The slow-drying colours allowed the artist to keep the painted image alive and moving by constantly redefining and overpainting. As shapes and colours became lost or blurred during the painting, they were continuously restated, emphasized and altered with yet brighter colour and stronger, more directional brushstrokes.

Alla prima

This direct approach to painting is sometimes referred to as 'alla prima'. Traditionally, alla prima means completing a painting at one sitting, but more generally it describes a fresh, spontaneous way of working – usually one which does not involve detailed planning or a preliminary drawing.

Broad brushstrokes and thick, impastoed colour are very typical of the alla prima method.

Knowing when to stop

There comes a point in any painting when it is detrimental to continue. For the inexperienced, it is all too easy not to recognize this point, and to carry on overworking by adding detail after detail.

In this case, the artist knew exactly when to stop. The flowers are left as rugged strokes of thick white, and the leaves as slashes of grey and green. Any attempt to add final detail would only have diminished and deadened the whole effect.

This painting did not progress gradually towards a predetermined finish. It remained in a constant state of change and flux until the artist felt the image was as vivid and dynamic as the subject itself.

◁ 1 *There is no preliminary drawing here. The artist made a few initial marks to indicate the position of the lilies and vase within the rectangular canvas, then immediately started to block in the colour. For this first stage, the paints were diluted with turpentine and applied thinly. The background is cadmium red. Sap green, cadmium yellow, black and cobalt blue are used for the flowers, foliage and jar.*

Although the paint is applied quickly with a large brush, the proportion and scale of each element are extremely accurate, and the artist looks constantly at the subject as work progresses. The canvas measures 36 × 24 inches (90 × 60 cm).

▽ 2 *The lilies are developed in thick, impastoed white. Brushstrokes look crude and unfinished as the artist strives to capture the bold, trumpet-like form of the lily. However, each stroke is precisely and confidently placed after careful reference to the subject.*

△ 3 *Occasionally paint becomes too thick in the early stages and can make further painting difficult. Excess colour is easily blotted off; here some of the thick white is removed with newspaper.*

△ 4 *The blotting has left the canvas free of excess paint and oil, while at the same time preserving much of the impastoed texture and the strong, directional blocking-in. This blotting technique is popularly called 'tonking'.*

▽ 5 *It is now time to overpaint and develop the blocking-in. More white is added to the lilies; foliage shadows are painted in strong sap green. The artist takes the leaf colour right up to the flowers, always looking at the subject and always redefining and clarifying the shapes as he works.*

△ 6 *The paint is now almost back to its original impastoed thickness, but this time the image is nearly complete and the textured paint is allowed to remain and form part of the finished painting.*

◁ △ 7 *Continuing with the background, the artist paints right up to and around the petals and leaves. Again, each is redrawn and redefined with the background colour.*

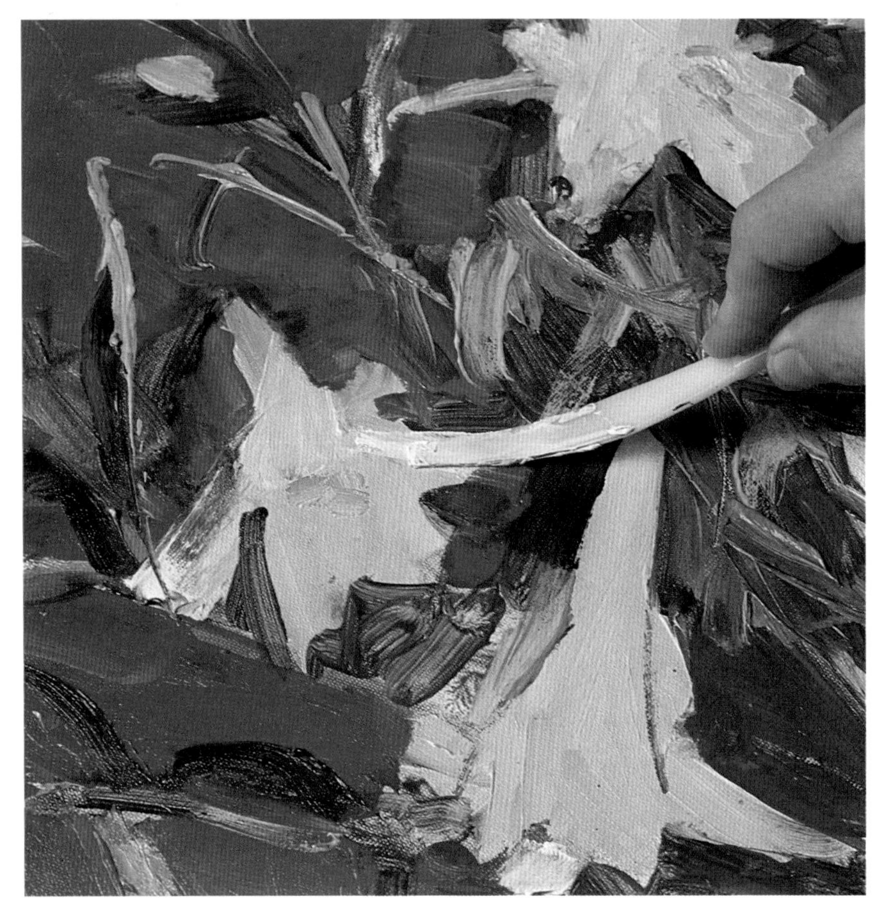

◁ 8 *Finally the lilies are built up with wedges of smooth white. The ridged texture is achieved by applying colour with a painting knife; spiky and jagged strokes are used to emphasize the long, spindle-like leaves and petals.*

▷ 9 *The picture is now complete. Further painting or more detail at this stage would destroy the freshness of the thickly textured paint surface, and weaken the strong, explosive quality of the lilies and leaves.*

PROJECTS

NARCISSI

Acrylic

Slavish detail is not necessarily the key to a realistic picture. Look at the finished painting of these narcissi. It is an absolutely fresh and naturalistic rendering of the flowers as they lie on the table, still wrapped in their tissue paper.

The first impression is one of near-photographic accuracy. Yet a closer look reveals that everything has been considerably simplified, and the realistic effect is something of an illusion. The light and dark tones of the leaves and flowers are reduced to a minimum, and each of these is left as a flat shape, with no attempt being made to blend or smooth it into the adjoining shape.

Acrylic is fast-drying, and this allowed the artist to overpaint and lay the areas of adjoining colour to achieve a clean, unblended image.

Composition

Another important aspect of this picture is the composition. Again, it is simple yet very effective. The rectangular canvas is divided into two main areas: the brown table-top and the white tissue paper. Each is painted as a strong, positive shape, and there is no sense of empty space or any feeling that the composition fades out towards the edge of the canvas.

Painting whites

Most whites have a bias towards a particular colour – often noticeable only when you see several whites close together. This is particularly true of white flowers. A bunch of different species of white flowers would soon show one to be creamy white, another to contain more pink or blue, and so on.

Too many similar whites in a subject can look chalky and dull, so it is important to observe and even emphasize the subtle colour differences. Here the white of the narcissi has a subtle cream tinge which accentuates the cold blue-whiteness of the tissue paper.

◁ 1 *A bunch of narcissi is arranged informally on a tabletop. The initial drawing is important because each bloom is seen from a different angle, and the artist wanted to establish the shapes and perspective before starting to paint. The drawing completed, he then blocks in the background with a mixture of black and ultramarine blue. This dark tone is the underpainting for the finished wood colour.*

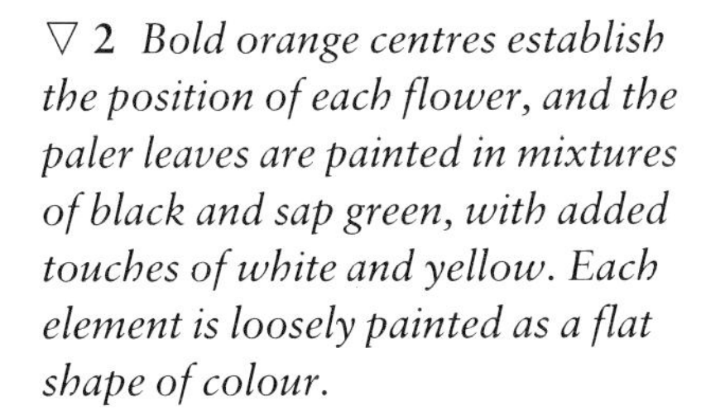

▽ 2 *Bold orange centres establish the position of each flower, and the paler leaves are painted in mixtures of black and sap green, with added touches of white and yellow. Each element is loosely painted as a flat shape of colour.*

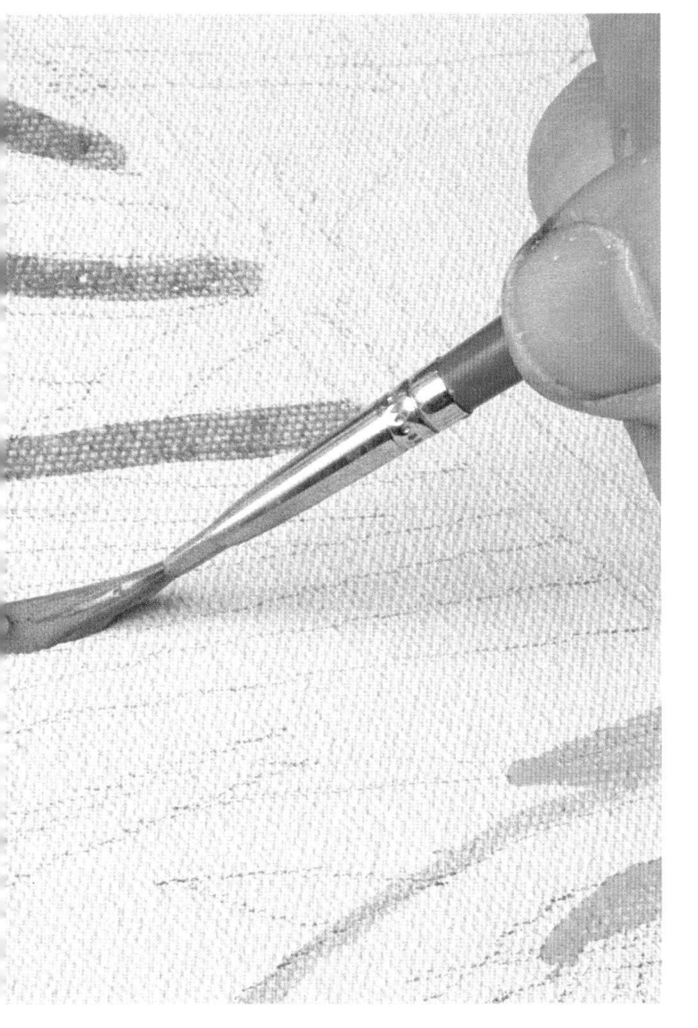

△ 3 *Still working in simple areas of colour, the stems are developed in light and dark tones of sap green, black, white and yellow. The tissue paper is blocked in with mixtures of white, black and cobalt blue, with the lightest tones being left white.*

△ 4 *Every shape in the painting so far has been simplified to its approximate local colour and tone. The narcissi at this stage are no more than shapes of white canvas, waiting to be developed. Yet already, because of the accuracy of the initial drawing and the closely observed colour, the unfinished painting is remarkably similar to the subject.*

◁ **5** *Grey shadows on the narcissi petals are painted in a basic mixture of white and raw umber. The cooler greys contain a little blue; the warmer tones, a touch of yellow ochre. Again, the paint is applied as flat patches of simplified colour.*

▽ **6** *The paler parts of the narcissi petals are painted in white with a touch of raw umber.*

△ 7 *Dark-orange shadows are applied to the flower centres in a mixture of cadmium orange and burnt sienna.*

▷ 8 *Apart from a few minor adjustments to the tones, the main subject – the flowers and the tissue paper – is now almost complete.*

△ **9** *After a careful reappraisal of the nearly completed picture, the artist feels the flower stems look too flat. This is corrected by adding one or two dark shadow tones where the stems disappear into the tissue paper.*

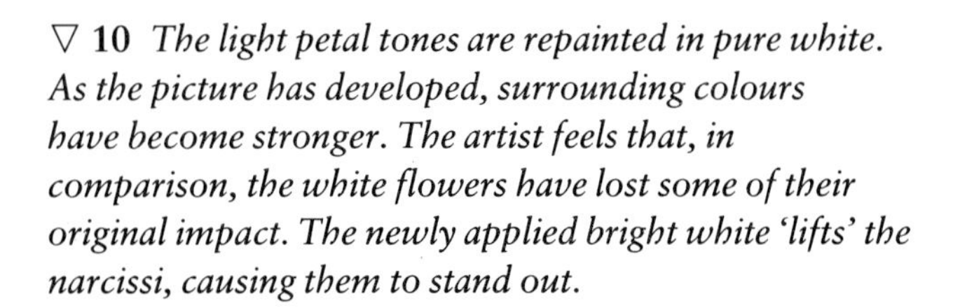

▽ **10** *The light petal tones are repainted in pure white. As the picture has developed, surrounding colours have become stronger. The artist feels that, in comparison, the white flowers have lost some of their original impact. The newly applied bright white 'lifts' the narcissi, causing them to stand out.*

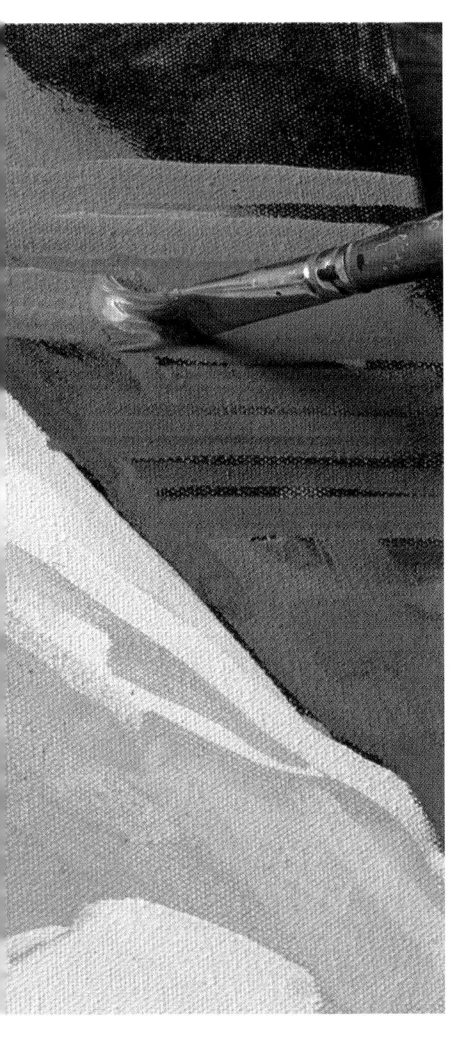

◁ **11** *Broad strokes of warm wood tone are laid across the tabletop, made from raw sienna, burnt sienna and white, mixed in varying proportions to obtain different tones. To achieve the 'wood grain', parallel strokes of colour are applied with a large, flat brush.*

△ **12** *The wood colour is taken up to and around some of the flower heads. This is done in bold, sure strokes, without changing the strong white petal shapes.*

◁ **13** *Seen from close quarters, the painting is clearly composed of tiny patches of separate colour. Each plane of light and shade is left as a flat shape, with visibly hard edges. Viewed from further away, the colours and tones merge into a perfectly formed and convincing image of a bunch of narcissi lying in their wrapping paper.*

CHAPTER 4 CHAPTER

Pastels

SOMEWHERE BETWEEN the drawing and painting media lie pastels, which can be used to convey linear qualities as well as to block in areas of colour. Pastels fall into two main categories: hard and soft. The hard pastels contain a lot of binder or wax. These, which include Conté pastels, are used mainly for drawing. Soft pastels are more crumbly. Within the soft pastel category there are degrees of hardness. Experienced pastel artists keep colours of various brands because they know exactly the subtle differences between them.

The colours of pastels are not mixed on the palette but are found in the shop. With paints you might have black, red and white on your palette, and from these you could mix a whole range of tones from very dark red to pale pink. With pastels you will find that the manufacturers have sought to produce as many of these tones as possible. This is because you cannot easily mix pastels before applying them, or blend them once they are on the paper.

Pastels smudge and so it is useful to 'fix' the finished picture. Fixative works like a fine varnish, holding the pigment particles in place. Fixing, however, darkens the colours, so should be used carefully. Some artists prefer instead to leave their paintings exposed to the atmosphere, which has a natural though less effective fixing property.

◁ **Dense colour** *A jar of pussy willow by Charmian Edgerton shows soft pastel at its brilliant best. Colours are merged and built up in close, dense strokes. The effect of light and shade on the leaves, catkins, and background is achieved with carefully controlled flecks of tone.*

△ **Light on dark** *Sally Michel chose a tinted paper for this pastel painting of flowers in a bowl. The subject is generally light, and the subtle pale colours show up effectively against a contrasting dark background.*

TECHNIQUES

BROKEN COLOUR

It is no coincidence that flowers are a favourite subject with many pastel artists. Pastels allows you not only to combine the linear quality of a drawing with the colour potential of a painting but also to produce the very brightest colours.

When oils or watercolours are mixed on a palette, some of the luminosity is inevitably lost in the mixing. With pastels, the colours are mixed in the picture, and this can be done without losing any of the vividness of the separate colours.

Optical mixing

Many Impressionists used paint in the same way that pastel artists apply colour: in order to get the brilliant colours of nature, they would apply pure or primary colours as separate blobs and allow these to mix optically, in the viewer's eye. Seen from close quarters, these paintings seem to be, say, a mass of bright-red, yellow and blue dots. Step back and the dots immediately become landscapes, flowers or figures painted in the colours of a brilliantly sunlit day.

Pastels cannot be pre-mixed. Either you have the exact colour you want or, more usually, you have to mix your colour optically on the paper. Thus a bright-green leaf can be made up of several different colours which combine optically to give the 'impression' of the actual leaf colour.

As you can imagine from these examples, the scope is enormous. Obviously, green is predominantly a mixture of blue and yellow, but there are so many different blues and yellows that different combinations of these in different proportions will

give an almost infinite variety of greens. A warm green will probably also include some red and brown; a shady leaf may include a lot of purple, and so on.

Broken colour *Pastel colours can be mixed by overlaying flecks or dots of pure pigment. In this illustration, yellows, blues, greens and pinks are combined to create a variety of 'leaf' colours.*

Colour opposites

Every colour has an opposite. If you remember the colour wheel, you will know that purple lies opposite yellow, blue opposite orange and red opposite green. If you place these colours next to or over each other, each one will seem brighter and more vibrant than if used separately.

The bright-red primula on page 73 is deliberately underpainted in green, the optical opposite of red. Flecks of green are allowed to show through in the finished picture, and the result is a truly brilliant red flower.

TECHNIQUES

PASTEL BACKGROUNDS

The background plays an important part in any flower painting, but this is particularly true of pastel, especially if you are working on light or white paper, as the artist does in the project on page 68.

With drawings and watercolour paintings, the background is sometimes deliberately left as a plain white area, against which the subject can be seen clearly and crisply. This is often the case if the work is of a detailed or botanical nature. But with pastel paintings, in which the colour is built up solidly and the texture of the paper can often be seen through the colour, the lack of a planned background will almost certainly make your painting look weak and unfinished.

Broken colour

If you use the classical pastel technique of broken colour – building up the image with flecks or strokes of separate colours – then build up the background in the same positive, solid manner.

In the illustrations below, various pastel paintings are shown alongside details of the background in each one. In every case the background colours include some of the colours used on the subject – the flowers and foliage. The result is a unity of colour throughout, and a background which is an

◁ ▷ The background to this arrangement of purple and yellow flowers is painted in strong vertical strokes of violet over a warm-orange underpainting. Substantial areas of orange are allowed to show through in the finished painting. This combination produces a particularly vivid effect. The violet of the background is picked up by the purples and violets in the subject.

integrated and important part of the whole painting.

The direction of the pastel strokes in the background can often be as important as the colours themselves. Bold vertical or horizontal strokes can provide an effective contrast to the natural, organic shapes of the subject. Conversely, you might decide to echo the natural forms of the subject by using the same curved or swirling strokes in the background. Another effective alternative is to do as the artist has done here in places, and to make the background strokes radiate outwards from the flowers, so concentrating the viewer's attention on the main subject.

Tinted paper

Instead of a worked background you may decide to use a tinted paper in the first place. Many pastel artists prefer to work on a medium-coloured paper, because this provides a middle tone against which the lights and darks can then be assessed. In other words, you can start straight away by blocking in the light and dark areas, the shadows and highlights, all of which show up on the paper, which then takes on the role of a middle tone in the painting.

The background will be better integrated if you allow flecks of the paper to show through the pastel strokes of the subject.

Choice of paper colour depends on the subject and the effect you want. For instance, a subject with lots of foliage could look good on a cool green, blue or grey background, which would pick up some of the colours of the leaves. Alternatively, you might deliberately choose a colour which contrasts with the green in the subject, such as warm brown or red.

▷ ▽ The background here is partially in deep shade, and this area is rendered in dark purple. A complementary bright orange depicts the sunlit side of the composition. In this painting the background colours reflect exactly those of the subject – orange and red chrysanthemums in a purple earthenware jar.

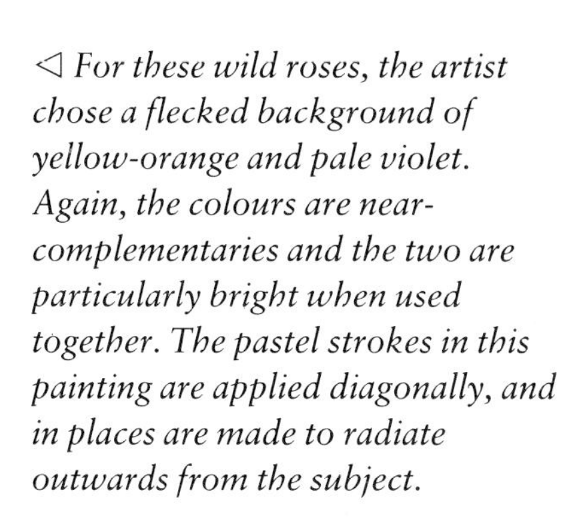

◁ For these wild roses, the artist chose a flecked background of yellow-orange and pale violet. Again, the colours are near-complementaries and the two are particularly bright when used together. The pastel strokes in this painting are applied diagonally, and in places are made to radiate outwards from the subject.

PROJECTS

POTTED PRIMULA

Soft pastel

Brilliant crimsons, gold, emeralds and rich violets are overlaid in this tiny, intensely coloured pastel painting. The picture measures no more than 8 inches (20 cm) square – a deliberately manageable size that enabled the artist to build up the colour gradually, using tiny strokes of dense pastel.

Colour with pastel

We have seen on the preceding pages how a colour can seem more brilliant when placed next to its opposite, or complementary, colour. Here the artist exploits this property to the full.

An exaggerated purple background – the real background is a dark wood colour – is introduced to set off the yellow flower centres. Green, the complementary of red, is used as an undercolour for the crimson and vermilion flowers. The whole effect is one of vibrating, shimmering colour.

In order to preserve the inherently brilliant pastel colours, it is necessary to keep the strokes separate. This means you should mix two or more colours by building up dense areas of flecks or strokes of each colour. If you attempt to mix pastel colours by blending or smudging them together, you will soon lose your vibrating colour effect and the result will be dull and muddy.

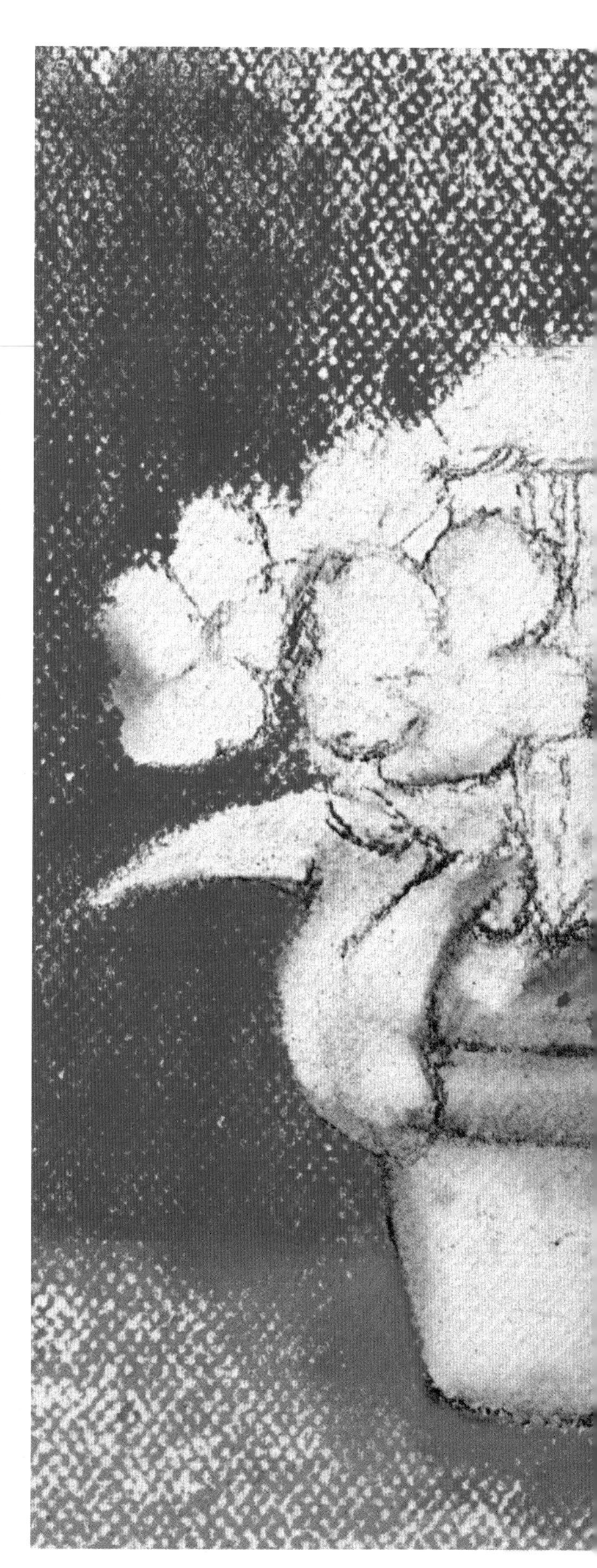

▷ **1** *Working on white Canson paper, the artist starts with a light charcoal drawing. The background is then blocked in with deep purple, interspersed with strokes of viridian green and cobalt blue. The picture area measures approximately 8 × 8 inches (20 × 20 cm).*

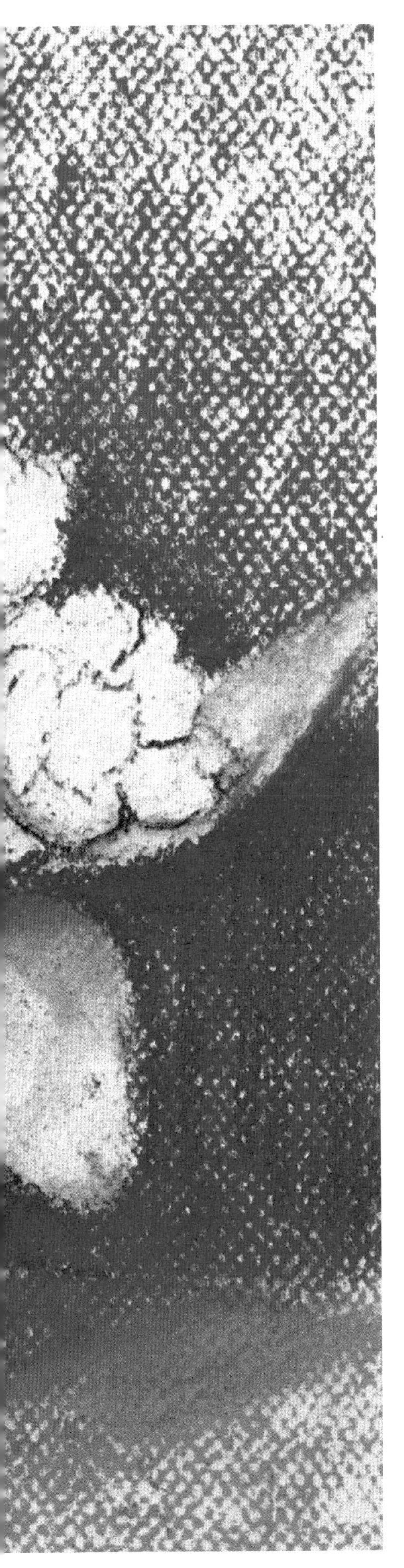

▽ 2 *The leaves are lightly established in two tones of viridian green, with touches of background purple in the shaded areas.*

▷ 3 *Eventually the flowers will be vivid red, but to achieve this final effect the artist starts with an underpainting of contrasting colours – light and dark turquoise for the petals and centres.*

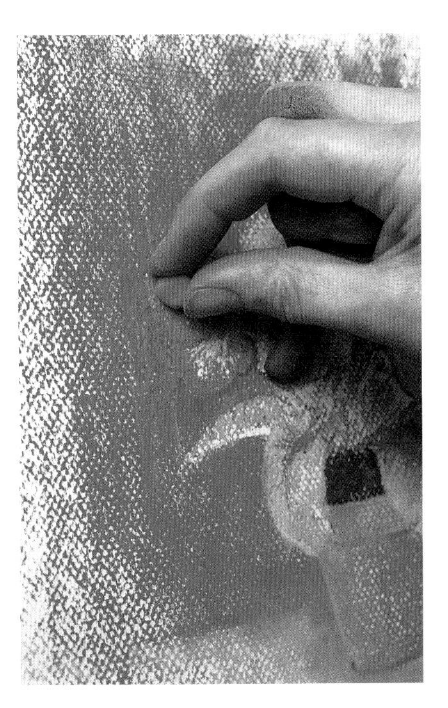

◁ 4 *The flower heads are painted in dense, overlaid strokes of alizarin crimson, vermilion and cobalt orange. The bright red of the petals is extended into the surrounding background in tiny, radiating dots – a technique often employed by the artist when painting flowers because it breaks up the otherwise hard edge of the petals. In this case, the optical mix of red and purple gives both colours an exceptional intensity and vividness.*

◁ 5 *Each flower centre is painted in yellow. Pastel yellows are often less intense than other pigments, and it can be difficult to build up dense layers of colour. To overcome this, the artist sprays the undercolour with fixative. This holds the pigments in place and makes the paper more receptive to further colour. Fixative tends to darken pastel, but spraying through a tissue mask enables the artist to fix the flower centre without affecting the surrounding colour.*

▷ 6 *Normally this artist avoids using fixative on a finished painting because of the darkening effect. However, in this painting she chose to fix the completed yellow flower centres to prevent the carefully built-up colour from smudging and losing its brightness. Still using the tissue mask, she has continued to build up flower centres to create bright, dense yellow.*

Pastel papers

The white Canson paper used here is specially made for use with pastels. It has a textured surface which holds the pastel particles and enables the colour to be built up in several layers.

But even specialist pastel papers have their limitations. Eventually the finely textured surface will clog and the pastel stick will start sliding across the overloaded surface. Occasionally the trouble-some area is quite small, in which case you can often carefully remove some of the excess built-up colour with a scalpel. For larger areas, try clearing the surface with a stiff paintbrush.

Depending on the brand, some pastels are extremely soft, while others are relatively hard. Soft pastels are very crumbly and tend to clog the paper more quickly than the harder sticks, which contain more binder.

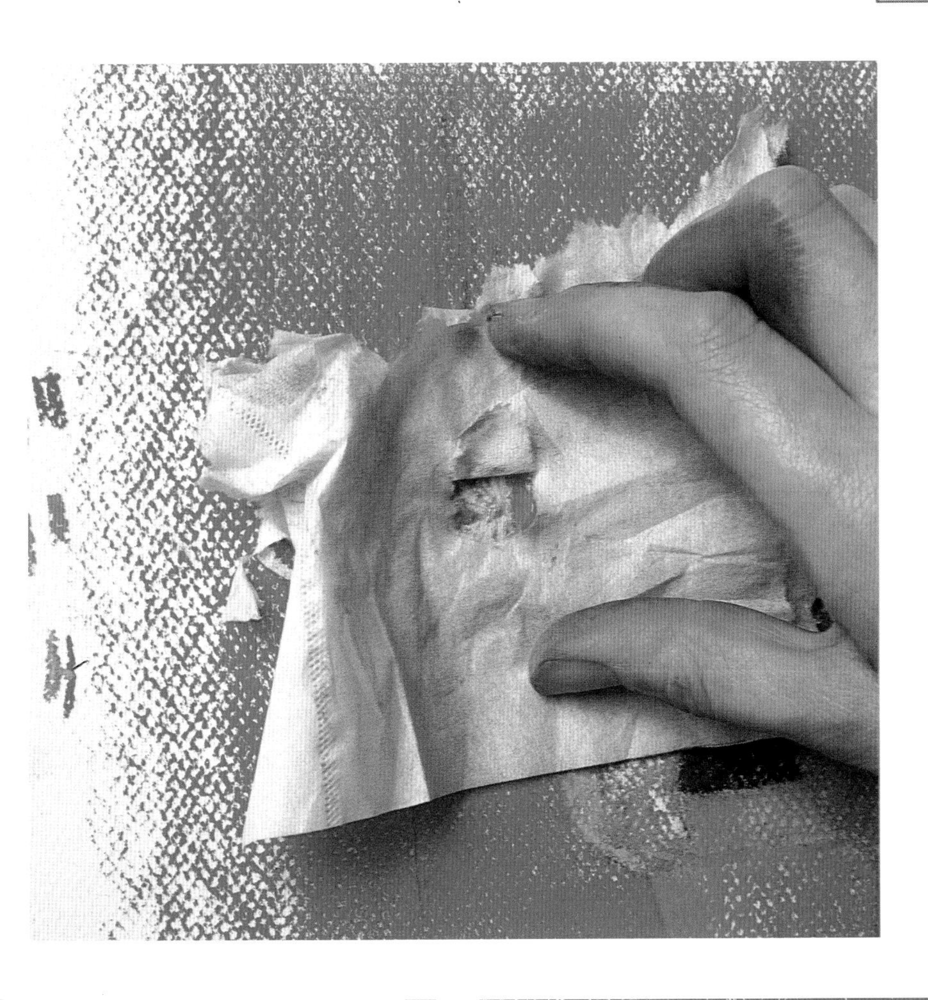

◁ 7 *Small corrections can be made by removing pigment particles with a stiff brush. Here the position of one of the flowers is being changed, and the artist brushes out the initial marks with a hog's hair paintbrush.*

△ 8 *The first three flowers are now finished. Although the colour is generally dense and bright, tiny patches of undercolour show through the final pastel layer, leaving specks of viridian and turquoise clearly visible.*

▽ **9** *The painting is nearing its final stage. Both the flowers and the background are complete; the leaves and the pot are ready for some finishing touches.*

▷ △ **10** *So far the leaves have been underpainted in two shades of viridian and developed with emerald green and light green to indicate the local colour. Veins are drawn in with strong ultramarine blue.*

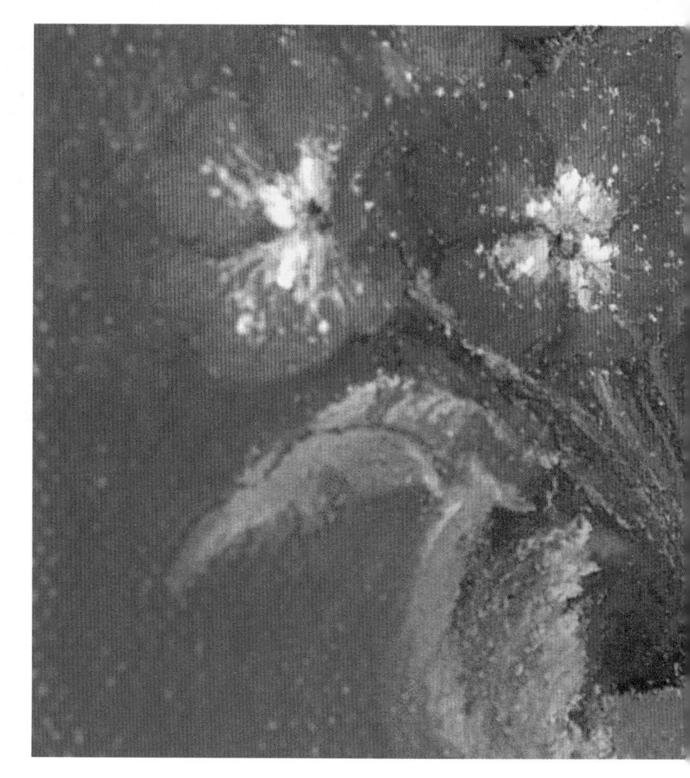

▷ **11** *The artist now goes on to work warm reds and pinks into the leaves, breaking up the hard outline of each with tiny dots of dark pink.*

△ **12** *In the finished picture, the blue and green underpainting of the plant pot is built up with warmer tones of brown, pink and red. The cooler colours of the underpainting show through, and deep purple is used to describe the shadows.*

CHAPTER 5 CHAPTER

Pencil and charcoal

The pencil is the modern equivalent of the 'silver point' used by Leonardo da Vinci (1452–1519) – a stick of sharpened silver which made its marks on a specially prepared sheet of coloured paper. Today's graphite pencil is capable of creating a broad range of marks, from the incisive line of the harder pencils to the broad lines and tonal areas of the softer ones.

With pencils, shading can be done with the side of the graphite point to get a soft, solid area. A more precise method of pencil-shading is 'hatching' or 'cross-hatching' – tiny parallel lines which can be overlaid, criss-cross fashion, to build up increasingly darker areas.

Charcoal is the perfect medium for the beginner. If you lack confidence, you tend to work too tightly and become overly concerned with particular parts of a drawing, to the detriment of the whole. With charcoal, this temptation is removed. The broad, chunky tip of a charcoal stick forces you to work in more general terms. This healthy approach will stand you in good stead, whether you continue using charcoal or move on to other media.

◁ **Watercolour pencil** *Watercolour pencil marks are watersoluble and, if wet with a brush, produce an effect similar to watercolour paint.*

▽ **Graphite pencil** *A well-sharpened 2B graphite pencil is versatile enough to produce a soft, dark line sufficiently precise to construct complex forms such as this teasle.*

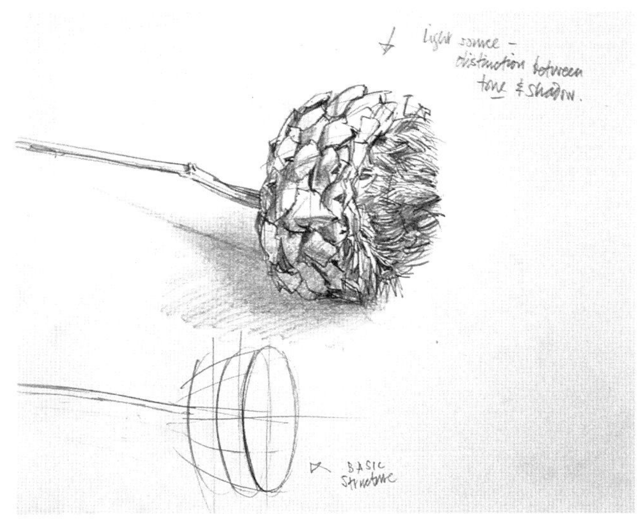

△ **Coloured pencil** *A useful drawing tool, coloured pencils can be used both for making lines and for rendering areas of light colour.*

PROJECTS

BLACK IRISES

Pencil

These subtle flowers, though beautiful, were not the easiest subject for a pencil drawing, because both flowers and leaves have a similar dark tone. The solution was a watercolour wash, giving a tonal background which enabled the artist to introduce some contrasting white in the final stages.

Drawing with pencil

Soft pencil is best for drawing because you can vary the thickness of line by altering the pressure on the pencil. A faint line is often better in the early stages, because it can be rubbed back and drawn over. The artist chose a 3B and a 6B.

It is important to keep the pencil well sharpened. You then have the option of using the point for fine lines or the edge of the lead for softer, broader lines.

Unless you are very experienced, it is best to start a drawing by measuring the subject and putting down some key marks on the paper. You can then move in, first with light, loose lines, and then developing bolder, more emphatic marks. There is more about this on pages 12 and 13.

Erasing is fine in moderation but should not be overdone, because too much rubbing out can interfere with the fluidity of the drawing. It is often better to alter a line by drawing over it.

Looking at the subject

Before starting work on these irises, the artist spent some time looking at the subject from different angles. This is good general practice, and especially so with flower arrangements, because it is important to understand not only the structure of the individual flowers but also the three-dimensional nature of the arrangement as a whole. Seen from just one angle, this can often look like a flat shape.

The only way to get a truly accurate drawing is to look constantly at the subject. It is there in front of you, so spend at least as much time looking at the subject as you do drawing it.

△ 1 *Black irises in a glass bottle are the subject of this pencil drawing. Both the flowers and the leaves are complex and subtle, with no strong contrasting local colours. The artist relied largely on line and minimal shading to describe the forms.*

△ 2 *Working on cartridge paper, the artist begins with a light watercolour wash, and allows this to dry. Using a 6B pencil, he then starts to sketch the flowers. The emphasis at this stage is on the direction and position of the main stems and blooms, which are indicated in light lines, with areas of tone to describe shadows.*

△ 3 *Remaining flowers are added, and the artist draws into the subject, defining the shapes and forms. Pencil lines and shading are kept to a minimum. Very dark tones are rendered in dense pencil marks; paler tones, with light cross-hatching. The light, medium and dark tones of the drawing relate exactly to the equivalent tones within the subject.*

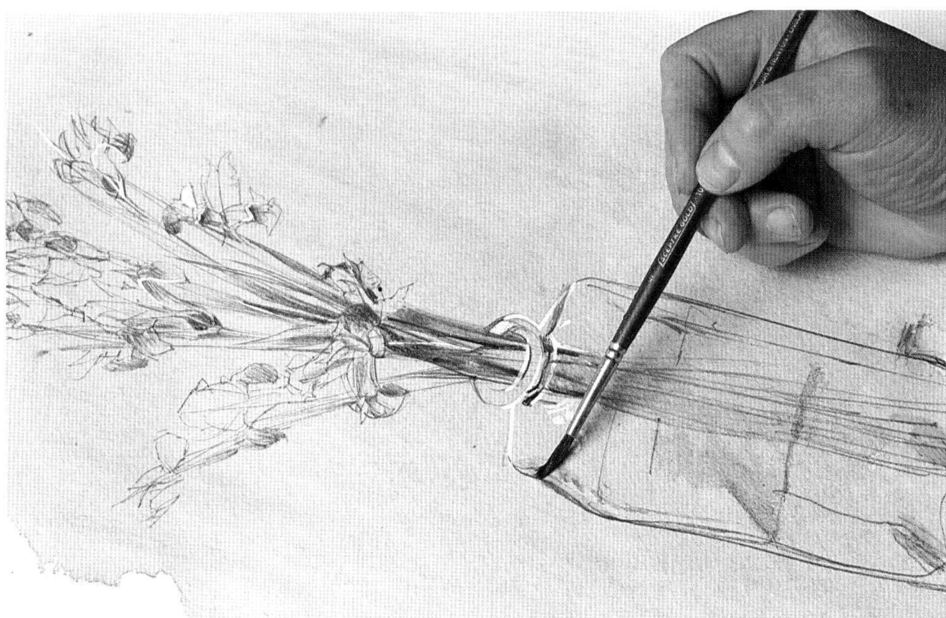

△ 5 *The botttle is drawn with a simple yet precise pencil outline. The main shadows and reflections are painted in black and white. Again, these are kept to a minimum, with just enough tone to describe the form and shape of the glass bottle.*

△ 4 *White gouache is used to emphasize some of the lighter areas, and these show up clearly against the initial background wash.*

△ 6 *Economy of line and tone is the key to this drawing. The artist referred continuously to the subject, often looking at the flowers as he drew, instead of at the drawing. Every line is accurate. There is no superfluous rendering and each mark has a purpose.*

PROJECTS

CARAFE OF FLOWERS

Charcoal

The flowers here are generally light in colour, and the pale tones are emphasized by the black velvet backcloth. The artist set out to make a tonal drawing, concentrating on the contrasting lights and darks rather than on the finer linear aspects of the subjects. Charcoal was ideal for this.

Drawing with charcoal

One of the best things about charcoal is that you can build up tones very quickly, often without making an initial line drawing. Here the artist started off with blocks of charcoal tone, then worked back into this with line to describe the form and shape of the subject.

Light tones can be added with white chalk or, as the artist does in this drawing, by rubbing back the charcoal to reveal the paler tones of the paper. Use a soft eraser, because this removes the soft dust without harming the paper. Failing that, white bread is a good alternative, especially when working on a large scale and rubbing out large areas.

Charcoal is compatible with chalk, and the two are often used together on grey paper. This effective way of making tonal drawings is very popular in art schools, as a means of encouraging students to see the subject in broad tonal terms before becoming concerned with rendering and detail.

Working big

One way in which charcoal really comes into its own is when you wish to work on a large scale. Use the bigger sticks for this – the types used by scene painters, like the one employed here. Apart from being rather fiddly to use, some of the finer charcoal – ideal for detail – tends to break easily if used with too much enthusiasm.

Paper for charcoal must have a surface with a certain amount of tooth. If you use very smooth papers, the charcoal slides around – which means you cannot achieve blacks and deep tones, or indeed very much tonal contrast at all. Sugar paper, cartridge paper or any of the pastel papers will work very well.

△ 1 *For this charcoal drawing, the artist wanted the subject to contain as much tonal contrast as possible. The black background emphasizes the pale tones of the flowers and glass jar, and was chosen for this reason.*

▽ 2 *The first stage shows the entire subject, first blocked in as a mass of dark tone, then rubbed back to show the broad, pale areas – the light flowers and leaves.*

▽ 5 *The finished drawing captures the complexities of cut flowers in a glass jar, using just a stick of charcoal and a piece of bread. By starting with the dark tones, the artist was able to work back to the white paper, creating shapes and highlights which were then defined only in the very final stages.*

△ 3 *Pale shapes are further defined by rubbing out more specific areas of charcoal. A kneadable eraser is suitable for this, or you can do as the artist does here and rub out with white bread. Bread leaves a clean surface and is especially good for removing large areas and bold shapes.*

▽ 4 *Finally the artist uses the charcoal to define the flowers and leaves with bold lines.*

CHAPTER 6 CHAPTER

Mixed media and collage

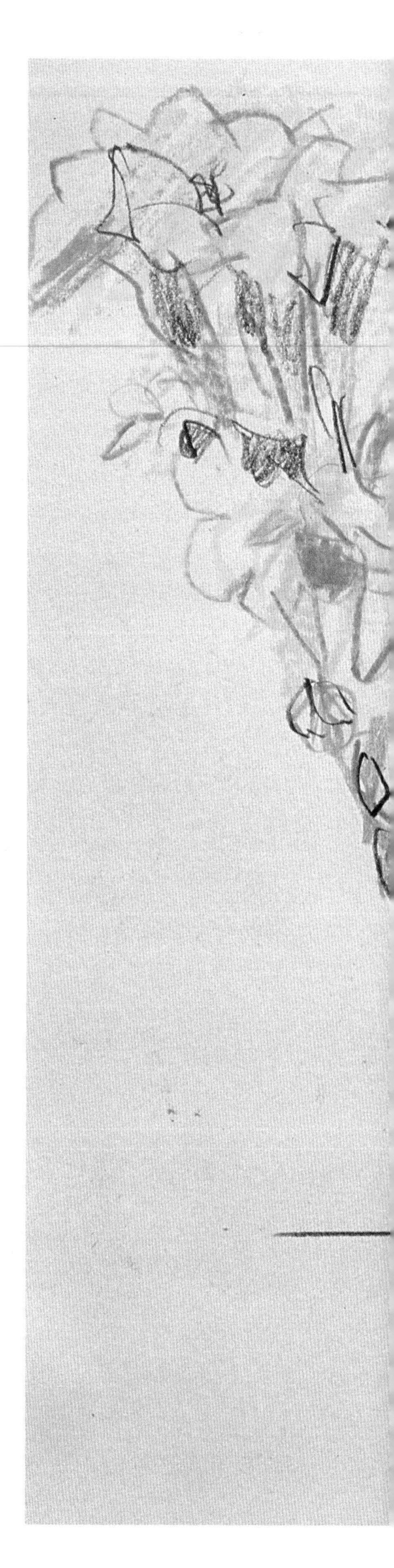

THE CHALLENGE of any subject is to capture the different elements in one image. Perhaps more than any other subject, flowers and plants are made of many elements. They have varied lines, textures and surface patterns. There is no reason why each of these very different elements should not be done in a different medium – the material which suits it best. Thus in the same picture you could use pastel for soft lines, dip pen for jagged edges, watercolour for pale washes and gouache or acrylic for strong colour.

Illustrators and graphic designers have been using mixed media for years. In fine art it has taken longer to break down the barriers. One of the most liberating factors is the invention of acrylic paints, used by professionals for half a century but only recently accepted as a paint for popular use. They can be used thickly or thinly, they dry rapidly and they are adhesive. The adhesive is strong enough to stick not only paper and card but also pieces of wood, plastic, metal and buttons, all of which have been used in acrylic collage.

Once you have explored the possibilities of collage and mixed media, your imagination is for ever stretched.

Pencil and paint *There is no reason why drawing and painting materials cannot be used together. This line drawing was done with a soft graphite pencil. The blooms were then boldly painted in yellow gouache and soft pastel.*

TECHNIQUES

TEXTURE WITH SCRAPS

The most exciting collage materials are often the most accessible ones. Obvious examples are waste paper, corrugated cardboard, newsprint and photographs. More textured results can be obtained with seeds, pulses, string, wools, woven materials, and so on. To avoid the frustration of not having the right materials to hand when you want them – this happens so often! – it is a good idea to start your own collection of bits and pieces now.

Scraps of paper, card, fabric and many other materials can be used to build up a collage picture. This may be done entirely in collage, or it could be a basis for further development with paint or any other medium.

Collage and paint
Excessive caution and timidity are common problems when embarking on a painting – and ones which are suffered by even the most experienced artists. Flowers and plants are often delicate and

Tone and texture *Collage made from newsprint, wrapping paper, tissue, handpressed paper, string, cotton, canvas, paint and chalk.*

detailed, and it is very easy to get carried away with detail too early and overlook the main shapes and forms. Starting off with collage, with pieces of toned, coloured and textured paper, is an excellent way of overcoming this problem, because it forces you to concentrate on the broad elements in the initial stages.

Collage also allows you to work out the main elements of a composition before sticking the pieces in their permanent positions. You can try different colours, tones and shapes by moving the components around until you are happy with the composition. Once the main shapes are down, you can then work into these with other media, such as watercolour, gouache or acrylic.

Tones, textures and colours of the initial collage elements can be incorporated into the picture. Or you may end up by obliterating the collage beginnings completely. The point is, the collage has served its purpose by starting the painting in a bold, broad and, hopefully, exciting way.

Acrylic and collage

You can use any paint when working with collage and mixed media, but acrylics are particularly well suited because the paints themselves are adhesive. This means you can apply an area of colour and then stick the collage pieces directly on to the wet paint. Acrylic media, which are colourless, are also excellent as strong adhesives.

TECHNIQUES

COLLAGE COLOUR

Torn and cut-out shapes have a graphic quality that cannot be imitated with paint or any other medium. But this does not mean that you can produce only stylized, graphic effects when working with collage. With skill and imagination, certain collage materials can be used to depict natural subjects in a highly realistic and subtle way. The results can be as simple or as sophisticated as you want to make them.

Be creative and experimental in your collages. The illustrations shown here were done with coloured tissue, photography, and a variety of coloured papers, but the possibilities are endless, and you will soon develop other techniques and a personal way of working.

Tissue paper

There is now a vast selection of coloured tissue papers on the market, with many of the colours also available in a range of tones. Tissue is very versatile – often more versatile than paint and pencil when it comes to capturing the different colours and shapes of many flowers.

When pieces of dry tissue are laid over each other the paper is deceptively opaque, but when the tissue is glued with acrylic medium or cow gum the colours become immediately more transparent, and you can build layers of brilliantly translucent petal

Paper collage *Flower picture made from magazines, coloured tissue, chalk and paint.*

and leaf effects in this way.

Tissue can be cut with scissors or torn. Cut edges are clean and hard, allowing you to be very precise with each shape. A torn edge, being gentler and more ragged, produces a defined but soft contour, similar to the delicate edges of many flower petals. In the illustrations below the artist has used both cut and torn edges to create the accurate but organic quality of the subjects.

Painted paper

Your collage need not be confined to commercially coloured papers, even though an enormous selection of these exists in the shops – and not only art shops. There is no reason why you cannot paint sheets or scraps of paper to suit your own requirements.

Manufactured paper comes in flat colours, and you may want a colour that is graded or textured. You can make this yourself with paint, crayon or whatever materials you choose. It is a good idea to paint or colour the paper before you cut it. This way, you will get a visibly torn or cut edge which will produce the effect of collage but at the same time give you absolute control over the colour.

Frottage

This rather grand name describes the process used by children when they get the impression of a coin by placing a sheet of paper over it and scribbling with pencil or crayon. It is also the method by which brass rubbings are obtained.

The same simple technique can also be used to give you a whole range of textured papers, which can then be cut or torn up and used in collage pictures. Any slightly raised surface will produce an all-over pattern or texture. Simply place a sheet of paper over the textured area and scribble across the sheet lightly with coloured pencil, crayon or pastel.

PROJECTS

FLOWER STALL

Collage

Every imaginable material has been used to make this colourful collage of the flower stall that stands in the street near the artist's home. Using so many materials made it impractical to work direct from the subject, so the artist started by taking a photograph. While this was being developed by the local fast-processing service, he went home to gather together as many coloured papers, paints and inks as he could muster!

Coloured paper

There was no preliminary drawing. The guides in this case were scraps of paper, torn to the approximate shape and size, and stuck down to establish the main areas of colour in the picture.

The most striking aspect of this subject was the abundance of brightly coloured flowers. But although colour is the main theme in the picture, it was not enough to work in coloured paper alone – the result would have been a flat design of unconnected shapes. A certain amount of texture, tone and line was needed to bring the coloured elements together.

Mixed media

You can use any compatible materials in a collage. For the flower-stand picture, the artist used gouache, watercolour and acrylic paints, as well as pencil, pastel and ink. Normally in a painting, the watercolour and gouache would not be used with acrylic, simply because gouache and watercolour are soluble once they have dried and acrylic is not – the painting techniques are therefore generally different for the two types of paint. But there is no technical reason why they cannot be used together in a work such as this.

Blobs of dark tonal colour were added in watercolour concentrate. This is an unusual way of using concentrates, because the colours are normally diluted with water, but here the artist specifically wanted the dark tone of the concentrated colour.

△ **1** *A coloured photograph was the reference for this collage picture. The artist 'sketched' out the subject and composition by sticking down torn scraps of paper to represent some of the strongest elements. These included tissue, art paper and one of his own discarded watercolour sketches.*

△ 2 Bunches of yellow flowers are added by dabbing gouache directly from the tube.

▽ 3 The initial shapes are drawn together into a cohesive composition. Gouache, watercolour and ink are painted between and over the coloured paper shapes, and more textural flower masses are dabbed on from tubes of acrylic and gouache.

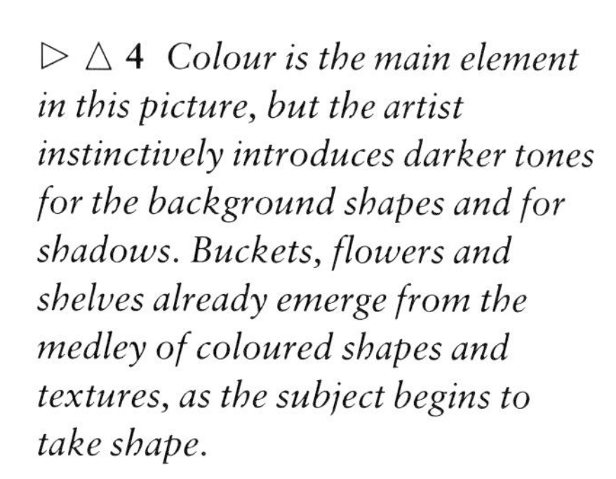

▷ △ 4 Colour is the main element in this picture, but the artist instinctively introduces darker tones for the background shapes and for shadows. Buckets, flowers and shelves already emerge from the medley of coloured shapes and textures, as the subject begins to take shape.

▽ 5 Floating blobs of abstract red, yellow and orange are transformed into background floral displays when the artist paints the black background shadows around them. The red awning, painted in watercolour, finally identifies the subject as a flower stall.

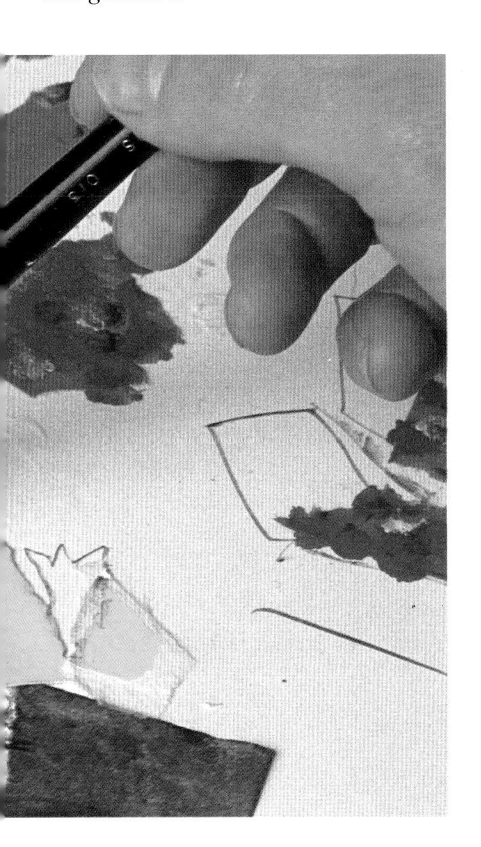

△ **6** *Undiluted watercolour concentrate, dropped on to the collage to form shadows under each of the colourful displays, seems haphazard. In fact, these shadows immediately transform the coloured shapes into three-dimensional elements and inevitably create an illusion of space on the flat paper.*

▷ **7** *Some final drawing is done with graphite pencil, coloured crayon and dip pen.*

◁ **8** *A close inspection of the collage shows at least part of this seemingly realistic image to be a clever illusion. We find splashes of colour and blobs of paint which are unrecognizable in themselves but immediately become identifiable as plants and flowers when the artist gives them a price tag!*

▽ **9** *Paper, paint, ink, crayon and pencil are all visible in the finished picture. The artist has exploited each material to the full, combining paper collage with painting and drawing techniques to recreate the many colours, textures and lines within this varied subject.*

PROJECTS

GOLDEN RANUNCULUS

Mixed media

Coloured pencil, ink, pastel and gouache all feature in this mixed-media painting. The materials were not especially planned but were chosen as the need arose. Gouache was perfect for the dense colours of the flowers and wrapping paper, pen and ink for the sharp definitions within the stems and foliage, and pastel for softer highlights of the paper.

The contrasting materials keep the painting bright and alive, giving the finished picture a spontaneity and freshness that often elude works done within the confines of a single medium.

Mixing materials

A 'mixed-media' picture is one that uses more than a single type of material. This is a broad definition, covering chalk used with charcoal, pen and ink with watercolour, and so on. Normally, however, it applies to more obvious mixtures, and frequently includes collage.

Cautionary notes

Most materials can be used together, but some combinations are easier and more suitable than others. Sometimes, of course, accidents are 'happy', and an unexpected result can be used to the advantage of the painting.

However, unless you specifically want the 'resist' effect of separated colours, it is essential to avoid using oils or oil pastels with other paints, because they emphatically do not mix.

Soft pastels, chalk and charcoal are all very versatile and look good combined with water-based paints. When using these materials on their own it is normal to apply fixative during the course of the work to prevent smudging. If you are combining them with paints, however, fixing can be done only in an extremely limited way, because fixative is a varnish and seals the surface of the paper; paint will not adhere to the shiny surface. If possible, it is best not to fix at all until the painting is finished.

You should also remember that some inks are waterproof when dry and others are water-soluble. If you apply water or wet paint to the latter, they will dissolve and run. As a deliberate effect, this is fine, but it is very messy when not intentional.

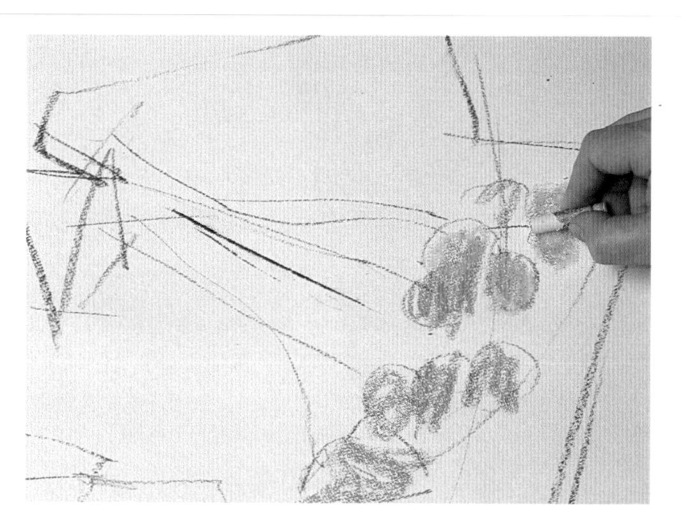

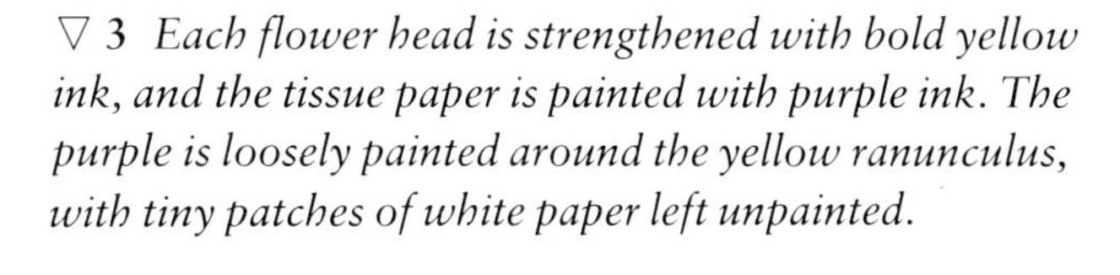

◁ ▽ **1** *Charcoal and soft pastel are used to sketch in the main shapes of this mixed-media painting. The artist set out a wide range of materials before starting work. When involved in a painting, he tends to use what is immediately available rather than stop and look for a particular material; the more materials to hand, the more varied the picture. His assortment included charcoal, soft pastel, coloured pencil, pen and ink, gouache and watercolour.*

▽ **2** *Each flower is scribbled in with pale-pink and yellow soft pastels. The leaves are painted with drawing inks, first in green and yellow and then, while these are still wet, with bold stripes of black. The black is allowed to bleed into the green foliage.*

▽ **3** *Each flower head is strengthened with bold yellow ink, and the tissue paper is painted with purple ink. The purple is loosely painted around the yellow ranunculus, with tiny patches of white paper left unpainted.*

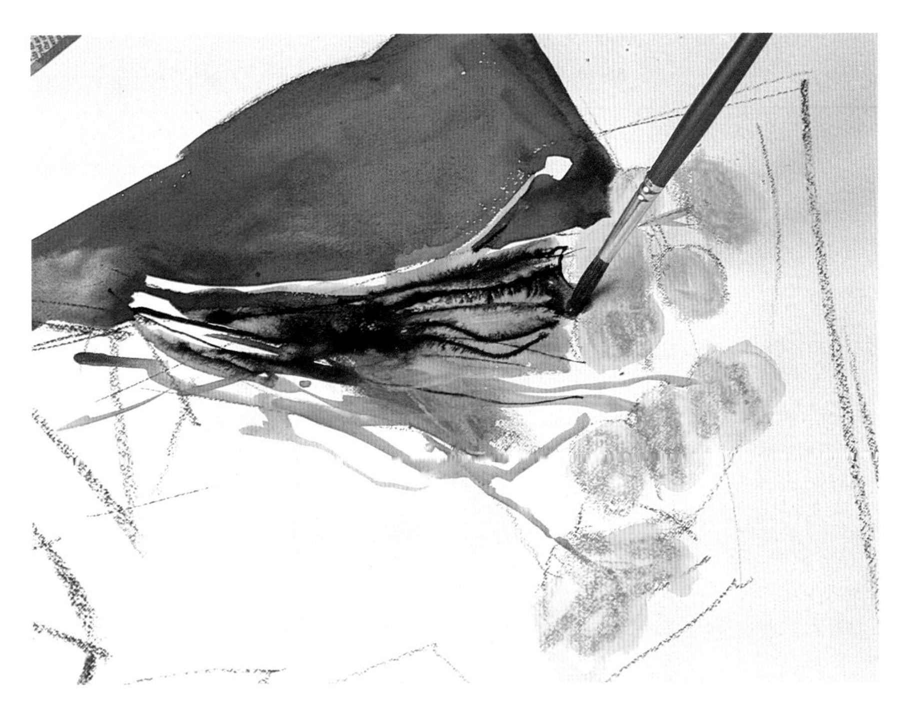

△ **4** *Darker tones of orange and red are painted into the flowers, using loose strokes of gouache and watercolour.*

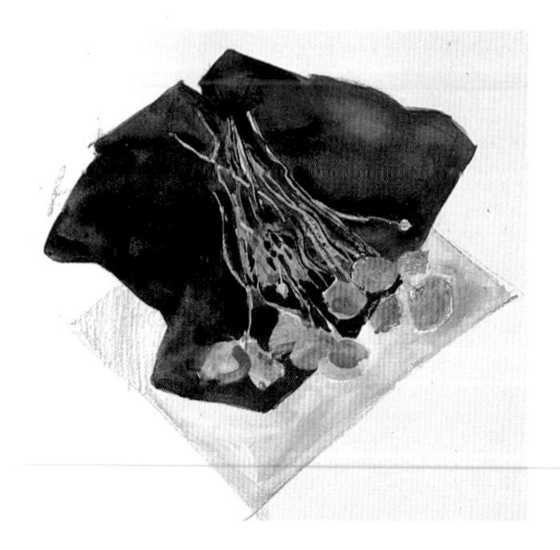

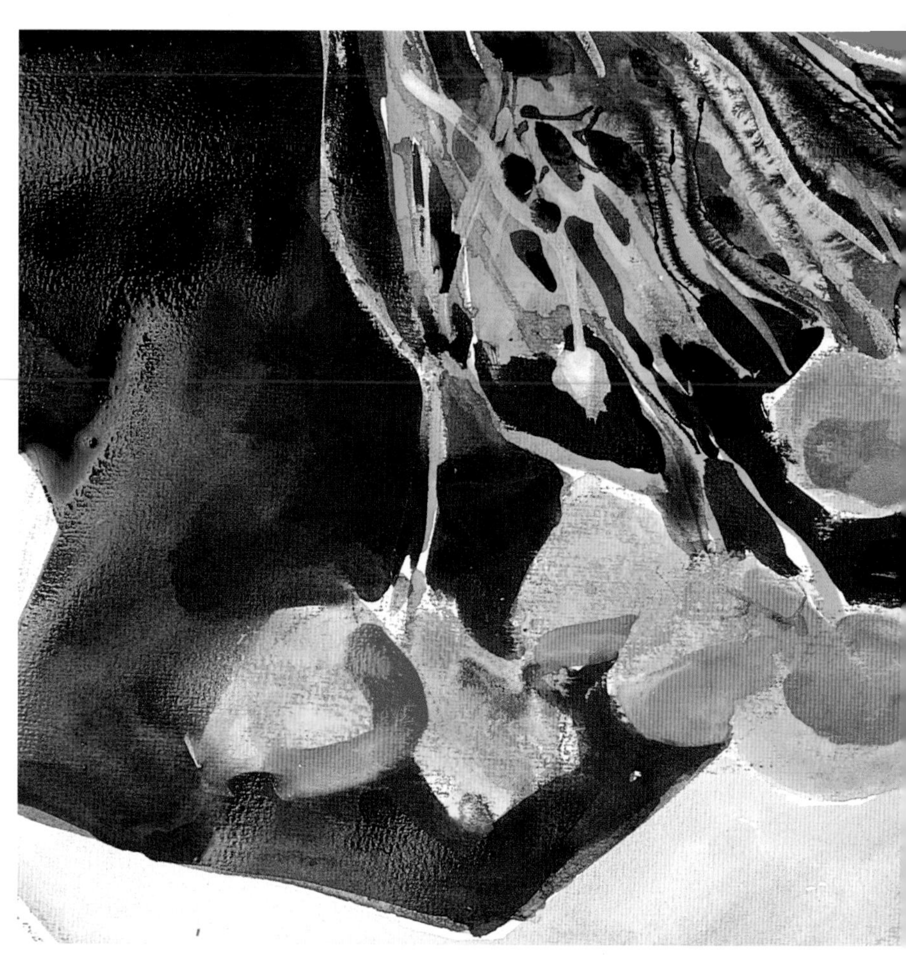

△ 5 At this stage, the artist has redrawn the stems using pen and ink, and redefined the spaces between the stems with a fine brush. The tabletop is established as a wash of brown watercolour, and certain flowers are darkened with patches of red gouache.

▷ 6 Increasingly deeper tones have been painted on to the original pale flower shapes. These depict the dark centres of the flowers and describe the shadows cast by certain petals.

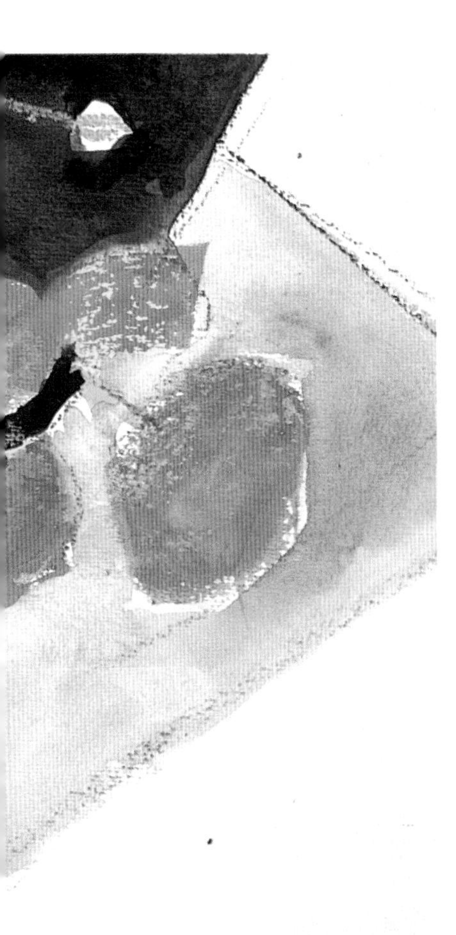

◁ 7 *Some of the flowers have been dissolved slightly with water to soften the strong colours. The artist then draws into the softer, dry shapes with a dip pen and brown ink to further describe the folded petals. The stalks are refined with pencil and white gouache.*

▷ △ 8 *The tissue paper is darkened with washes of black and stands out as an emphatic shape. Reflected light on the purple tissue is sketched in with pale-violet soft pastel.*

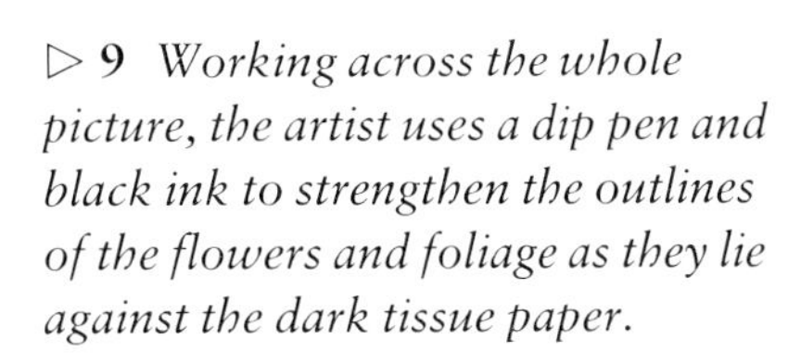

▷ 9 *Working across the whole picture, the artist uses a dip pen and black ink to strengthen the outlines of the flowers and foliage as they lie against the dark tissue paper.*

△ **10** *Dark-red, scratchy ink lines complete the flowers. The leaves are added in bright-yellow gouache, applied in feathery strokes with a fine brush.*

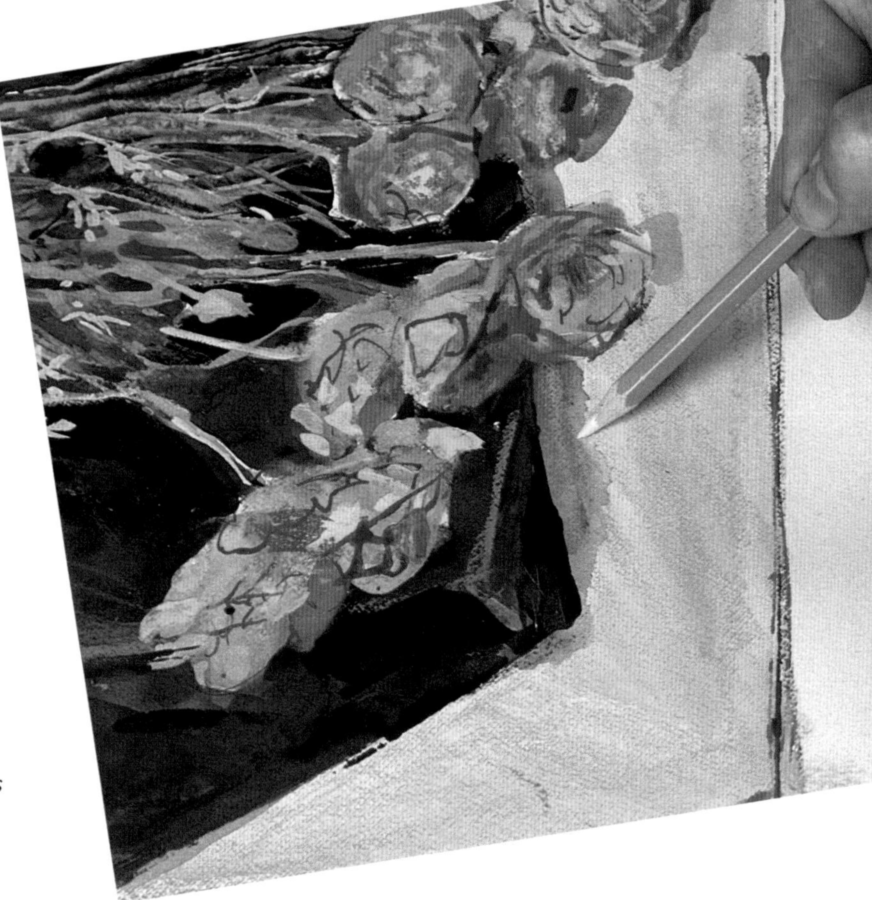

▷ **11** *Brown, yellow and orange coloured pencils are scribbled across the table surface to give the impression of wood grain.*

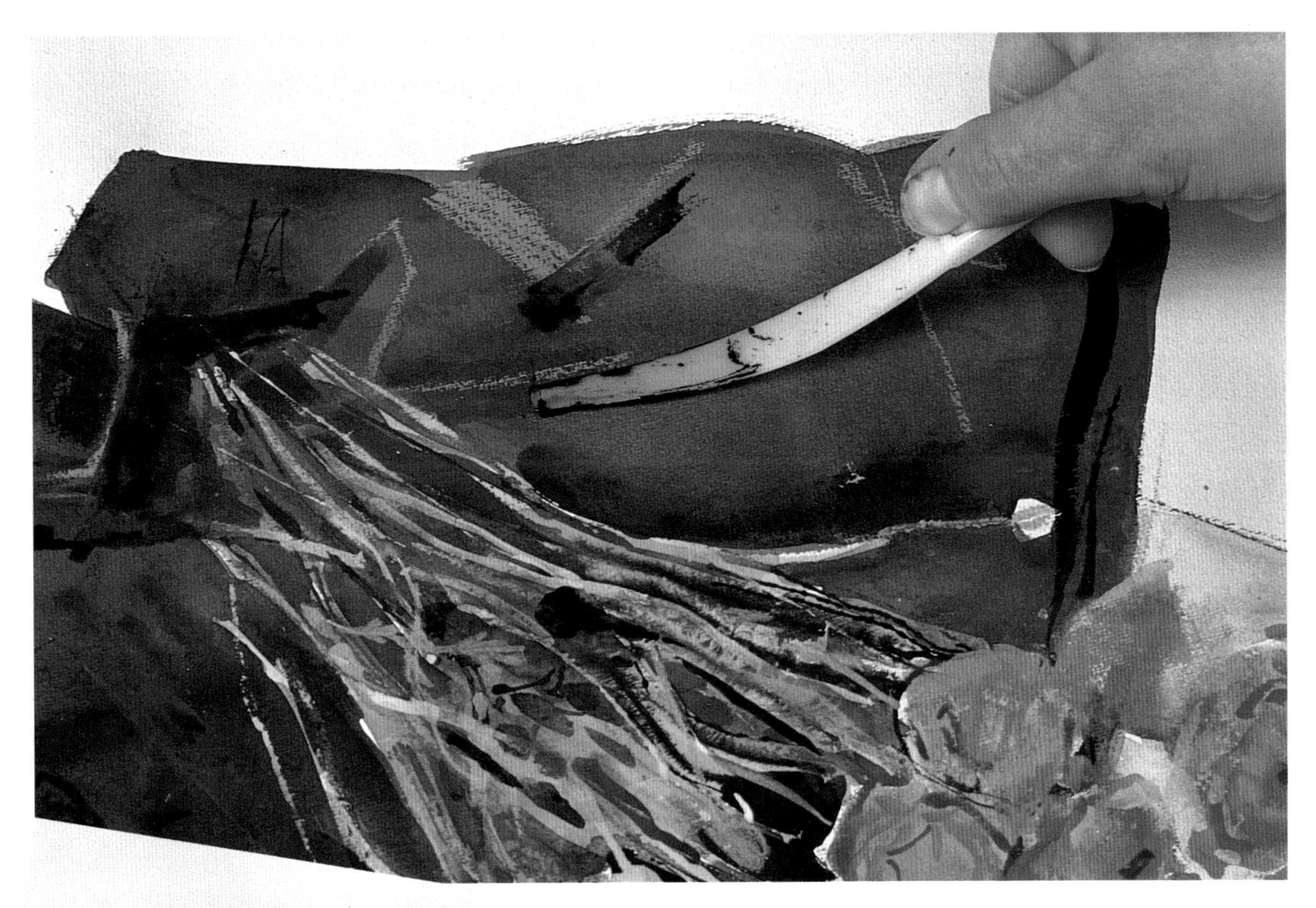

△ **12** *A few final touches of pale pastel accentuate the highlights on the tissue paper, then dense, deep shadows are added with a palette knife.*

◁ **13** *The many different colours and textures within the subject have been recreated in this lively and experimental mixed-media painting. An unusual number of art materials were incorporated into the picture. More important than these, though, was an artist with an open mind and a willingness to experiment with all the materials available.*

INDEX